To - Anna Bomgardner
From - Cora Ebersole
Birthday May 29, 1963

How to Build a Happy Home

HOW TO BUILD A HAPPY HOME

by

B. CHARLES HOSTETTER

Pastor and Director,

THE MENNONITE HOUR International Broadcast

ZONDERVAN PUBLISHING HOUSE

GRAND RAPIDS, MICHIGAN

How to Build a Happy Home

Zondervan Publishing House
Grand Rapids, Michigan

Second printing – 1962

Printed in the United States of America

PREFACE

Christianity is not out of date. It is the practical life to live in our time, in any time. It has provisions for all of our needs. It has help for every problem. Since family life is of great importance, God through His Word has given us a lot of suggestions and guidance on HOW TO BUILD A HAPPY HOME.

To a great extent the future of a nation will be determined by the kind of homes it has. The home is God's first institution and the most important one. Unhappy, unspiritual and broken homes are the breeders of most of the vices and pave the way for crime and wickedness of all kinds. Happy home building is a *must* for good communities and strong nations.

Much credit for our happy home must go to my sweetheart and faithful wife. God has blessed our home with eight children, but in spite of her busy schedule as mother, she finds time to encourage me in the ministry of the Gospel. She has helped me, inspired me, and given me wise counsel. God bless her for her many sacrifices and for shouldering the added responsibilities occasioned by my absences. She is indeed a main carpenter in our happy home building.

The material in this book has been in preparation during the twenty-one years I have been married and a minister. But for the most part, this material was first put into writing to be used on the international broadcast of THE MENNONITE HOUR on which I serve as pastor.

Preface

I pray that these suggestions and Biblical truths may continue to be a blessing as they have now been collected and revised into this form. *How to Build a Happy Home* is dedicated to mankind for God's glory.

B. Charles Hostetter
Pastor and Director, The Mennonite Hour

CONTENTS

How to Build a Happy Home

I

GOD INSTITUTED MARRIAGE

Kin Hubbard said, "Women are just like elephants t' me. I like t' look at 'em, but I don't want one." But as I know men, that's a rare attitude. Both men and women have a "built in" attraction for each other. Love between the sexes is a normal experience in human relationships.

The Bible says that "God created man in his own image" (Genesis 1:27). Man was the highest of God's creation, even more important than angels. He was to be a son of God and was to help rule part of the universe. God said to Adam, ". . . subdue it [the earth]: and have dominion over the fish of the sea, and over the fowl of the air, and over every living thing that moveth upon the earth" (Genesis 1:28). Man was not created to live a selfish life; his purposes and goals were tied with God's. And woman was made to be man's companion and helper. After God created the first man, Adam, He said, "It is not good for the man to be alone; I will make him a suitable helper, completing him" (Genesis 2:18, Berkeley).

We see from the origin of the human race that God made male and female for each other. Man needs woman and woman needs man. They have an affinity for each other. The two sexes are complementary, and when joined together in marriage they become one, because God binds them together.

The wise Solomon said, "Whoso findeth a wife findeth

a good thing, and obtaineth favour of the Lord" (Proverbs 18:22). But one husband I read about felt there were some exceptions to Solomon's statement. He found a wife but their marriage was unhappy. Finally, to get away from his nagging mate, he joined the army. But her letters to him brought him no cheer because she only complained and criticized. At last the husband wrote to his wife saying, "Honey, please don't write to me so often. I want to enjoy this war in peace!"

To make marriage a success, one must understand its true nature and God's purpose for it. There is much more involved in marriage than the fifteen or twenty-minute ceremony. Many marriages fail because the divine objectives for them have been ignored. It is futile to try to make marriage a success apart from the Creator's laws regulating it.

What is the purpose and nature of marriage and what are the laws that govern it? We find the Biblical doctrine of marriage imbedded in the first chapters of the Bible. "And the Lord God formed man of the dust of the ground, and breathed into his nostrils the breath of life; and man became a living soul. . . . And the Lord God said, It is not good that the man should be alone; I will make him an help meet for him. . . . And the Lord God caused a deep sleep to fall upon Adam, and he slept: and he took one of his ribs, and closed up the flesh instead thereof; and the rib which the Lord God had taken from man, made he a woman, and brought her unto the man. And Adam said, This is now bone of my bones, and flesh of my flesh: she shall be called Woman, because she was taken out of Man. Therefore shall a man leave his father and his mother, and shall cleave unto his wife: and they shall be one flesh. . . . And God blessed them, and God said unto them, Be fruitful, and multiply, and replenish the earth, and subdue it" (Genesis 2:7, 18, 21-24; 1:28a).

The Scriptures tell us that marriage was not a program inaugurated by God to accommodate man's appetites after he fell into sin and received a depraved nature. Marriage was instituted before the fall of man. It was a part of God's original plan. Man and woman were designed to be counterparts. Love between sexes is a normal experience in human relationship and is not a mere convenience. Marriage is not a custom which gradually became accepted in early human history. Neither is it a mere temporary, manmade arrangement that exists for social convenience. Marriage is God-ordained and the laws regulating it are tied to God's judgment and eternity. So when man ignores and breaks the divine rules regulating it, he will suffer for it here and in the hereafter, unless he repents.

Jesus also had much to say about God's purpose in marriage. He reveals that the original divine program still stands. "The Pharisees also came unto him, tempting him, and saying unto him, Is it lawful for a man to put away his wife for every cause? And he answered and said unto them, Have ye not read, that he which made them at the beginning made them male and female, and said, For this cause shall a man leave father and mother, and shall cleave to his wife: and they twain shall be one flesh? Wherefore they are no more twain, but one flesh. What therefore God hath joined together, let not man put asunder" (Matthew 19:3-6).

The partnership created through marriage is more intimate than any other human relationship, even that of parent and child. The Bible says that at marriage the bride and groom shall leave their parents and cleave unto each other because they have become one flesh. The root meaning implies that they are firmly fastened together as by welding. They are bound together, the two becoming one. It is an organic union that comes out of the depth of life.

The importance and permanence of marriage is to be

found in this uniting experience. It is a physical, spiritual and mystical union of one man and one woman joined together by God. Two men or two women could never experience this unity. It is the blending of male and female virtues and characteristics that produces a oneness which no physician, scientist or philosopher can explain. The marriage union is a great mystery, but a thrilling reality when it is formed in the Lord.

Marriage is more than a civil contract. It constitutes a bond that only God can bind. It makes each person infinitely more than he or she could ever be alone. Husband and wife are to complement each other. In the first marriage, Adam said, "This is now bone of my bones, and flesh of my flesh" (Genesis 2:23). Two souls are united into one, to live life together as one unit. The Apostle Paul says, "So ought men to love their wives as their own bodies. He that loveth his wife loveth himself" (Ephesians 5:28). That's why a husband (or wife) will sometimes speak of his "better half."

Today, however, marriage is not popularly considered as two persons becoming one, nor is the commitment to each other until death. Rather, it is thought of as a social convenience, to meet certain temporary conditions. Marriage is often used to serve selfish objectives, and in such cases it is entered into or discarded at will. The accepted code set forth in our modern novels, movies, stage, radio and television is far below the code that God established. This explains why many marriages have been failures. No alteration by human law affects the eternal law of the Almighty. The Lord does not change His principles to accommodate man's whims. When man disobeys God's laws, he reaps the consequences.

God provided marriage for man's happiness. It was designed to be a blessing to man. When you achieve its purpose that God ordained, you will have a personal, intimate and satisfying experience. Professor Edwin S. Burdell, of the Massachusetts Institute of Technology declared in commenting on Census Bureau Statistics showing (1) the alarming number of suicides among single men; (2) the lower death rate among married men; (3) that fewer married men go insane, and (4) that fewer commit crimes: "Marriage is the best insurance in the world – insurance against crime, insanity, poverty, and premature death."

It's true that the Bible says, "Whoso findeth a wife findeth a good thing, and obtaineth favour of the Lord" (Proverbs 18:22). But this is not an unqualified promise. Most of God's promises are only fulfilled when we meet certain conditions that He has laid down as prerequisites. To illustrate: God told the unfaithful high priest Eli, "I said indeed that thy house, and the house of thy father, should walk before me for ever: but now the Lord saith, Be it far from me; for them that honour me I will honour, and they that despise me shall be lightly esteemed" (I Samuel 2:30). Here God withdrew His promised blessings because Eli failed in meeting God's requirements.

In the same way, if you want your marriage to be a success and if you want your home to be happy, you must live within the framework of God's will and laws. If you honor God in your marriage and home, God will honor you. But if you neglect to do this, failure, unhappiness and regret will result. Give your life to Christ unreservedly and let Him turn your failures and sorrows into peace and happiness. Jesus said He has come to give us the abundant life (John 10:10). So we must yield to Him before we can build truly happy homes.

II

HAPPY HOMES DON'T JUST HAPPEN

Years ago when our two girls were little, they came home from the last day of school and cleaned and rearranged their bedroom. After it was all tidy, they decided they would play with their dolls. They announced to their mother that they were going to play "real" mother and "real" baby.

They laundered and ironed their dolly clothes. Then they washed their little feeding bottles and filled them from a can of evaporated milk they purchased from their mother. These bottles were then placed carefully in the refrigerator.

At bedtime they came running for the alarm clock. Upon questioning them we found that they wanted to get up to give their babies 2:00 and 6:00 a.m. feedings. We informed them that mothers took their babies off the 2:00 a.m. feeding as soon as possible. Yes, they knew that, but they told us their babies were just "borned" yesterday. So the alarm was set. At 2:00 a.m. they jumped up and ran downstairs to heat two little bottles of milk. After feeding their doll babies they took the bottles down to the refrigerator again.

Being "real" mothers and having real babies lasted only a few days, but the experience tells us something of how God made us. Even in little girls the mother and home instinct begins to express itself. It is a natural desire for us human beings to get married and to build homes. It is the dream of a normal person to marry someone he loves and to have a happy home. The Lord designed us that way.

But having a happy home doesn't just happen. You might accidentally drift into a love affair, but not into a happy marriage. Getting married is easy. Millions do it every year. But the marriage ceremony has no magic that transforms people. One is no different in character after the wedding day. Building a happy marriage takes planning, skill, effort, and most of all, divine help.

God's original purpose in male and female is to unite them through love and holy matrimony. This is the best and happiest relation for man and woman, because it is ordained of God. Of course, we know that it is God's will for some to remain unmarried. Our Lord and the Apostle Paul are examples of this. Under such circumstances supreme happiness and usefulness can be attained without marriage.

However, all through the Bible we find a sanction upon marriage. The Scriptures assume the husband-and-wife relationship to be normal and encourage the experience, but under the proper conditions, of course.

Proverbs 18:22 says, "Whoso findeth a wife findeth a good thing, and obtaineth favour of the Lord." In Proverbs 31: 10, we read, "Who can find a virtuous woman? for her price is far above rubies." In the New Testament marriage is also commended. I Timothy 5:14 says, "I will therefore that the younger women marry." And Hebrews 13:4 declares, "Marriage is honourable in all."

Even though God ordained that marriage and home building should be a delightful experience, many marriages end in separation. Far too many couples end up with broken homes when they should be building happy homes. This is one of the great tragedies of our generation, and it is blighting and cursing our society. How long will it be until we learn and acknowledge that defying the laws of God brings bitter reaping?

God has planned that the average person should get married, and that this is to be a happy relationship. Everyone wants to arrive at living happily ever afterward, but seemingly few care about following God's directions to get there. It seems that many have the mistaken idea that they can ignore and despise God's high standards and still get good results. That is impossible! You are being deceived if you for one moment expect to build a happy home while you ignore God's program for home building. You can't beat the Author of marriage at His own game. Regardless of what you think or plan, you are doomed to failure, living outside the program of God. You may be getting along just fine now, even though you are defying God's laws that govern marriage, but all the chapters are not yet written. "Be not deceived; God is not mocked: for whatsoever a man soweth, that shall he also reap. For he that soweth to his flesh shall of the flesh reap corruption; but he that soweth to the Spirit shall of the Spirit reap life everlasting" (Galatians 6:7, 8).

A little illustration, often used to teach children the lesson that one must start right to end right, would fit here. When you start wrong to button your jacket, you end wrong. However, if you put the first button in the first buttonhole and take them in proper order, then you have a proper ending.

In the same way God guarantees a happy home if you start right and follow His directions. An unhappy home is the result of either starting wrong or else starting right but getting out of the will of God along the way. Is your home unhappy? Has your home gone to pieces? Then you must begin where you are and with God's help and direction put the pieces together again. You may yet have a happy home. The cracks may always be visible, but with a determined effort on the part of husband and wife and the guidance of the Lord, your home can succeed.

The happiness of husband and wife determines the kind of home the children will be born into. The character, happiness and eternal future of the children hinge considerably on the kind of home they are reared in. And the success of a home determines whether its contribution is good or evil to the community, and even to the nation. Beyond that the eternal destiny of parents, children and even grandchildern may be determined by the happiness or unhappiness of a home. Unhappy homes have often driven their members into sin and wickedness of all kinds. Having an unhappy home is the beginning of tragedy that probably never ends in exerting evil influences. It has a harmful effect on every individual and every group that the family touches.

Here are some principles that underlie successful home building. If you are not yet married and if you and your partner-to-be will follow God's formula all the way, then you are guaranteed a happy home. If you are married and your home is not as it should be, we pray that this will help you to see some reasons for your difficulties and will help you to correct them.

Next to being saved, the most important decision a person makes is his choice of a life companion. So much is at stake in getting married that we should take no chances.

Young people, enter into your courtship and marriage seriously; be sure to let God lead you in each step. Never compromise with lust. Beware of the devil-inspired program that makes a joke of purity and tries to delude you with the idea that one is popular and up-to-date if he indulges in the social sins of our day. Satan would make us feel out of date, puritanical and old fogyish to live by the high moral standards of the Bible, yet those who are living up-to-date by compromising and rejecting God's ideals are certainly reaping a harvest of misery and unhappiness. If the proof of the pudding is in the eating, then those who are living by God's formula have no apologies and are ready to compare results with the world and its lust-inspired program. One can't win true happiness in social life outside the principles of God's Word.

These are days when much pomp and elaborate display are associated with weddings. But little is planned of the sort that would help make the marriage endure. If you took away all the artificiality, the veneer and the show, you would have little left at many weddings, that is Christ-honoring. The serious purpose to bind two lovers together for a lifetime of home building is entirely lost in lavish display. Getting married is a happy occasion but a serious one. It is to be a spiritual experience, not a time to demonstrate pride.

According to the high percentage of broken marriages and unhappy homes and the alarming increase of unfaithfulness to the marriage vow, it would appear we too often sing the wrong songs on the wedding day. We sing "O Perfect Love," "I Love You Truly," and "O Father, Lead Us." It would appear more appropriate to sing such songs as "Sound the Battle Cry," or "The Fight Is On," or even the song, "Once More Before We Part." If it were not so serious, it would be humorous.

Just getting married does not guarantee success. Even marrying someone you love does not assure you happiness. Many a person has wrongly assumed that if he marries a Christian or a person from a good, respectable family, he will be sure to have a happy home. It takes more than that; God's plan must be followed. Also forethought and serious planning by both bride and groom are essential to have a successful marriage.

There is fun and excitement in planning to go on trips, arranging for the first date, planning for college or marriage. But after the excitement of the planning is over, one discovers that he must have foundation principles and must work persistently to make the program and plan a real success. We are aware that arriving on a college campus and enrolling as a student does not give one a college degree. One must work, plan and put forth effort. In the same way, both husband and wife will have to give themselves to the task of loving one another and making their marriage a success. Marriage will be disappointing for both unless they put their all into it. It will not succeed on its own momentum.

Do you wish your home to be a happy one? Jesus Christ came not only to save our souls but also our homes. Give Christ His rightful place in your life and home and you will discover He will perform a miracle in it and bring happiness there. May God give you courage to do this.

"One of the first acts of the last emperor of Germany after his coronation was the dismissal of Bismarck, the great chancellor, who had made Germany what she was. Shortly after, there appeared in the London *Punch* that famous cartoon, 'Dropping the Pilot.' It pictured a ship starting out to the stormy sea. On the deck was the captain, the young emperor. A little boat was alongside, and the pilot, Bismarck, was going down the ladder. William was dropping his pilot. From that hour Germany was riding to destruction. Whatever you do, you who are just starting on the matrimonial sea, or you who are half over, do not drop the pilot."[1]

To stay married you must keep God at the helm of your home.

[1] Stuart Nye Hutchison, "The Sacredness of Marriage," *Christian Monitor* (February, 1944), p. 47.

III

ESSENTIAL ATTITUDES FOR SUCCESS

There seems to be a deep-rooted idea that when one gets married, he finds happiness ready made. Nothing could be farther from the truth. A successful marriage costs something. It's a test of character. No one is born a good marriage partner; he must pay the price of being one. The happiest marriages are those in which people do what they can to make each other happy, instead of using each other to make themselves happy.

Let's be realistic – no one ever marries the angel he dreamed about. All men and women have feet of clay. If you had found and married the angel of your dreams, you wouldn't feel at home with her anyway. Her perfection would condemn you in your imperfections. The differences between you would be too great. We all have failures and need forgiveness. So it takes the force of true love to blend two different personalities into one happy union. Such love is more than vague emotion or a romantic sentiment arising from admiration and attraction.

The old proverb says, "When you run in a double harness, take a good look at the other horse." A permanent marriage is one in which the two people involved have common ideals and goals, loyalty, complete trust and courtesy. Also there must be a determination to make marriage a success. Most of all, it takes a deep affection for each other and vital Christian living on the part of both partners.

Some children were forced to play inside because it was raining. The living room was the scene of their activities. After some time had elapsed, their mother heard them quarreling, getting louder and louder. Quickly she stepped to the living room to referee and to tell them that arguing and quarreling are never the way to settle differences of opinion. The mother's lecture had just started when one of the children informed her that they really were not cross at each other – they were just playing mother and daddy.

In the light of all the divorces, broken homes, lawsuits, and headline stories in the newspapers, we must conclude that in many homes it is far too common to have arguments and quarrels. This is not the way God wants it to be, but when homes are not built on spiritual foundations and Christ is not the head, trouble is invited.

There is no other human association so intimate as that of husband and wife, and, perhaps for that reason, no other so difficult. Therefore, it is tremendously important that the laws which bring success in this human relationship be observed. Having a courtship and a marriage ceremony does not guarantee happiness. We must face the fact that marriage, to be a success, requires sacrifice, unselfishness, and thoughtfulness, as well as love and planning. The same principles that apply in friendships apply in marriage, only to a greater degree.

Jesus lays down one of the most basic principles for success in human relationships in the Golden Rule, and this is a *must* for building a happy home. He says, "And as ye would that men should do to you, do ye also to them likewise" (Luke 6:31). If husband and wife will live and work for the interest and welfare of each other, a large span is bridged toward making that home a happy one.

Professor C. B. Eavey in his excellent book, *Principles of Personality Building for Christian Parents,* gives an idea that has been a blessing to me ever since I read it. He suggests that happiness is a by-product. When people go out just to find happiness for themselves, they never find it. But if they seek it for others, their efforts return happiness to them. In other words, if you want to find happiness you must seek for something higher than your own happiness. One gets it as a reward incidentally, as a result of love and service to others.

Husband and wife both receive happiness if each will observe this Golden Rule of Jesus. Happiness is not possible if only one observes the rule. It is when one or the other becomes selfish, wants his own way and works for his own interests, that trouble and unhappiness result.

While this principle of unselfishness is important within the family itself, it is no less important for family happiness in community relations. If a family has only personal interests, and everything is geared for its selfish success, then trouble and unhappiness will also come in inter-family relationships. Here then is a great secret for happiness in life: Live for the glory of God and the success of others and you will receive in return happiness for yourself.

A lawyer one time asked Jesus which was the greatest commandment. Jesus said, "Thou shalt love the Lord thy God with all thy heart, and with all thy soul, and with all thy mind, and with all thy strength: this is the first commandment. And the second is like, namely this, Thou shalt love thy neighbour as thyself. There is none other commandment greater than these" (Mark 12:30, 31). These "greatest" commandments of the Bible are ignored and violated by many among us, and we then wonder why our homes fail and why there is so much trouble and unhappiness in the world? When we get back to honoring God and living obediently to His Word, then we will get the by-products of Christian living—joy and happiness—not before.

Another law for building a happy home is continuing the spirit of courtship all through married life. Love, if it is to grow, must be nurtured. It must not be taken for granted, even after marriage. I am certain that many homes become unhappy because the thoughtful, loving and winning program used during courtship was unused or even misused not long after the wedding day. The practices that are important in winning love are no less important in maintaining it. If neatness, courtesy, thoughtfulness and unselfishness are fundamental in nurturing love during courtship, they are fundamental in preserving it. Let us keep in mind that the marriage vows in no way change our personalities; therefore, these practices are important and essential after the honeymoon. Let me repeat, this principle is important for both husband and wife to remember.

It is possible for a person to be loved now and despised later. To be loved today does not insure future affection. Love must be developed and nurtured. You can expect unhappiness and dissatisfaction in your home if you are now taking each other's love for granted. If either husband or wife has become careless in appearance, in habits, in courtesies, and if kindness and love are no longer practiced, then likely your home is in trouble. Love is being destroyed and you can expect more unhappiness ahead.

Love is something that can be experienced but not adequately explained or defined. It is intangible, but nevertheless real. One of the characteristics of human love is that it must receive love in return in order to grow. A wife's love for her husband cannot increase unless he returns her love, or vice versa. In fact, love will slowly die unless it is nourished by love. It does not operate on a one-way street. Therefore, to build a happy home, intimate love must exist between husband and wife, and the rules for developing and nurturing love must be followed all through married life. To state it more simply, keep up noble courtship practices throughout life. Husband and wife should continue all through married life to love each other as Christ loved the Church. Love dare not be ignored, but must be nurtured. To fail in this point is to set the stage for an unhappy home.

It doesn't take much to cause friction. "Many a married couple is like a team of horses, separated by a tongue." It takes Christian virtues to blend two personalities into one unit. Therefore a mighty preventive to broken homes is regular Bible reading and prayer in the family, plus regular church attendance. It takes God's grace and power to stay happily married.

The doorbell rang. When I opened the door I stood facing a middle-aged man. He had his overcoat collar turned up and because it was early dawn, I had difficulty seeing the man's face. He was a stranger to me.

He began by asking if I was busy. I told him I was a minister and was preparing several messages to be preached later that day. "Yes," he said, "I know you are a preacher. I have heard you speak several times – that is why I have come to see you."

I invited him in to talk. He unburdened his heart and told me a long, sad story of his broken home. He and his wife had been settled in their occupation, had been church members, and had a family. Much to his surprise, one day his wife left him and the children because of interest in another man. After some effort she secured a divorce and married the other man.

Now it was years later and his wife had just separated from her second husband. He wanted me to try to persuade her to come back to him, which I promised to do.

In the course of the conversation he told me he had lost out spiritually and was seldom attending church. I tried to show him that his first and most important step was to get right with God. He could not hope to secure the Lord's help in solving his home difficulty so long as he was out of fellowship with God. I reminded him that "The Lord is far from the wicked: but he heareth the prayer of the righteous" (Proverbs 15:29). He was not even in a position to pray to God about the problem because he wasn't on praying terms. The Bible says, "The effectual fervent prayer of a righteous man availeth much" (James 5:16).

My visitor wasn't interested in dealing with his sins and getting peace with God. He argued that he wanted to be reconciled with his wife first and then they would consider getting right with God and going back to the church.

He was just like many more people; they get the cart before the horse. During courtship and early marriage they have no interest in spiritual things. Oh, yes, they feel that Christ is essential and the church is important, but they will not concern themselves with those things until later in life, perhaps after some children are born; then they will have to settle down anyway. This is indeed a mistake. Because of the eternal implications, every home should be planned and operated upon spiritual foundations from its very beginning.

One needs the guidance and help of God to find his life partner. Also, those first years of married life are crucial because they often set the pattern for later married life. It happens over and over that the first ideal plans never get carried out. There are many broken hearts and unhappy homes today because the promises and plans made during courtship and early marriage were never fulfilled. It is the same old story—people play with fire and expect not to get burned. If you won't let God lead you from the beginning, your disobedience will bring unhappy consequences. You can't ignore God's laws for a time and escape the reaping.

Put it down, God means what He says. If you want to reap the fruit of God's leading, you must follow Him from the beginning.

As far as I know my visitor was never reconciled to his wife. He, like many others, wanted God's results without using God's methods. You can't get them! He had his own way, but he also reaped the fruit of his own way. This is an unchangeable and inescapable law of God.

Jesus said, "Seek ye *first* the kingdom of God, and his righteousness; and all these things shall be added unto you." To build a happy home you must put first things first. Jesus promises that if we will build our homes on spiritual foundations, seeking first the eternal values, then our homes will be blessed of God. In courtship we need to let the Holy Spirit guide us, and we need always to have high ideals and standards. Then we need to put Christ at the head of our homes from the wedding day on if we wish to have happy homes.

Often people have little or no interest in spiritual things until their homes are about to be broken, or else sickness or tragedy comes. But God isn't interested in operating on an emergency basis only. The Lord wants people to love and serve Him faithfully every hour of the day and every day of the year, not just when they are in a jam or a crisis from which human effort can't deliver them. How long would you respond to pleas for help if time after time your advice and counsel were ignored, mocked and rejected? We have Scriptures that tell us that God isn't going to be a puppet to man, always helping in the emergency, if His spiritual laws go unheeded at all other times.

Are you indifferent to God's Word? Are you building your home with no concern for its spiritual foundation? Are you ignoring the conviction of the Holy Spirit, the burden of your conscience, the counsel of the church and the truth of God's Word? To so live will bring you bitter experiences ahead. When your reaping catches up with you, God may not then choose to be an emergency deliverer for you. God addresses these most sobering words to those who are practicing sin without concern. He says, "Because I have called, and ye refused; I have stretched out my hand, and no man regarded; but ye have set at nought all my counsel, and would none of my reproof: I also will laugh at your calamity; I will mock when your fear cometh; when your fear cometh as desolation, and your destruction cometh as a whirlwind; when distress and anguish cometh upon you. Then shall they call upon me, but I will not answer; they shall seek me early, but they shall not find me: for that they hated knowledge, and did not choose the fear of the Lord: they would none of my counsel: they despised all my reproof. Therefore shall they eat of the fruit of their own way, and be filled with their own devices" (Proverbs 1:24-31). This passage of Scripture says that God is not mocked; He isn't a tool that can be picked up or discarded at will.

The Lord made abundant provision for us to build happy homes. He stands ready to help us and is eager that we enjoy the best in this world and in the world to come. His services can be had without money and they are available for all. But He does demand that we be His disciples. The key that opens the door to God's blessings and benefits is discipleship. If we love, obey and serve God, He is always ready to assist us with life's duties.

In family life there are many important decisions to make, decisions that have lifetime, even eternal, consequences. If we have a Christ-honoring home, then God will help us make those decisions. Proverbs 3:5, 6 says, "Trust in the Lord with all thine heart; and lean not unto thine own understanding. In all thy ways acknowledge him, and he shall direct thy paths." What a privilege that a Christian can build his home with divine guidance! This assures success.

Building a home is perhaps the greatest task anyone will ever have. If you will build your home upon spiritual principles, God is ever present to assist you. "The angel of the Lord encampeth round about them that fear him, and delivereth them" (Psalm 34:7). Or notice this great promise, "As the mountains are round about Jerusalem, so the Lord is round about his people from henceforth even for ever" (Psalm 125:2). As home builders we certainly need this divine help, because there are many evil influences that are stalking our lives and families to ruin them.

Are you planning on building a home? God wants it to be happy. But you can't build a happy home without the help of the Lord. Use the Scriptures as your source book for guiding principles and you will succeed.

IV

THE HUSBAND'S PART

One time Jesus was passing through the city of Jericho and great crowds encircled Him as He went. Zacchaeus, one of the rich citizens who was head tax collector, was eager to get a look at Him. He was too short to see above the crowd, and so he finally ran ahead and climbed up a tree along the street Jesus was taking.

When Jesus came to the tree, He looked up and said, "Zacchaeus, make haste, and come down; for today I must abide at thy house." Zacchaeus climbed down quickly and received Him joyfully. He then began to confess his sins and desired to make restitution. Then Jesus said to him, "This day is salvation come to this house."

A Sunday school teacher of little folks taught this story of Zacchaeus one Sunday to her class. The next Sunday, for a review, the teacher asked if anyone could tell the story.

One little fellow raised his hand. He got along well until he came to the part where Jesus stopped at the tree and invited Zacchaeus to come down, so he could abide at his house.

The little storyteller said, "So Jesus stopped on His journey and went over to the big tree where Zacchaeus was hiding and Jesus said to him, 'Zacchaeus, Zacchaeus, come down – or I'll huff and I'll puff and I'll blow the tree down.'"

The little boy got his stories mixed. He took parts of two

stories and changed the real meaning and lost the spiritual lesson.

In the same way many folks get married and start building a home and they never get a happy one because they mix the formulas. If in your home building you mix part of the world's formula with God's formula, don't expect to get God's results. Only with the divine program are you guaranteed a happy home.

The wedding is to be a spiritual experience. Husband and wife are to remember that God joined them together. From the wedding day on, family worship and attending Sunday school and church should be regular features. And each should live an exemplary life, challenging the other to noble and vital Christian living. A prerequisite for an enduring marriage is giving the spiritual life first place in the home. If Christ is not the head of the home and if God and His Word are not honored, then the stage is set for unhappiness.

One of God's chief laws for building a happy home is to have each member of the family filling his or her place as prescribed in God's Word. When we get our responsibilities mixed and one member plays a wrong part or one member fails to fulfill his or her part, then the story of that home doesn't end right, just like the little boy's version of the Zacchaeus story.

Let's go to the Scriptures and find out the responsibilities that God has assigned to husband, wife and children. If your home is not happy, check; perhaps you have some duties wrongly arranged or someone is shirking his God-given responsibility. As another has said, "Home is the father's kingdom, the mother's world, the children's paradise."

First, let's look at man's part as a husband in the home.

Here are some basic responsibilities we have as husbands:

1. Making the marriage a partnership.
2. Assuming the role as senior partner and high priest of the home.
3. Loving the wife as Christ loved the Church.
4. Providing a normal sex life for the wife.

As we look at these four responsibilities briefly, may God search our hearts as husbands and help us to make any adjustments necessary. If we want our homes to be happy, we must be obedient to the principles of God's holy Word.

1. *Making Marriage a Partnership*

In my judgment Ephesians 5:21 is the beginning of the paragraph concerning the duties of husband and wife. Here Paul says, "Submitting yourselves one to another in the fear of God." Jesus said, "For this cause shall a man leave his father and mother, and cleave to his wife; and they twain shall be one flesh: so then they are no more twain, but one flesh" (Mark 10:7, 8).

Many homes are unhappy because the husbands do not function as partners with their wives. Often men are quick to quote the Bible verses that say, "Wives, *submit* yourselves unto your own husbands" or, "The husband is the *head* of the wife." They fail, however, to see these verses in the total picture or context. Husband and wife through marriage become one flesh and they now submit themselves to one another in the fear of God.

Wives do not become through marriage servants, slaves, puppets or outlets to satisfy lust. Woman was not taken from man's head for him to lord over her; neither from his foot for him to kick around, but from his side to become his partner to help him with life's responsibility. Neither was woman made to fulfill the selfish desires of man. The home is not to be geared to carry out a program for the husband's happiness alone; it is to be geared for the greatest happiness of the whole family.

It appears at times that some husbands have the idea that all the wheels of the home should turn for their pleasures. They spend the money largely on themselves, go to places and do things for their enjoyment, have the household run to fulfill their comfort and desires. The fact that we men are the wage earners gives us no right to spend the money as we please or to have a larger proportionate share.

One of the principles for building a happy home is to make marriage a partnership. No one of the family should live selfishly or feel superior. Husband, is your home run on a partnership basis? If not, correct it. It is basic in God's program for making happy homes.

A young man was married while in college. He planned little for his wife's happiness. His studies and part-time employment came first. Their whole program was geared for him. She was to work every day in an office and do the household duties in the evenings. He had little time for love and seldom planned for her happiness.

She finally left him, got a divorce, and remarried. This tragedy ruined his career. He has had one disappointment after another since. As I listened to his story, I felt his mistake was that of not making his marriage a partnership. Now his former plans and dreams have all vanished and his training is unused. Men, we are to become one flesh with our wives and submit ourselves to each other. Our leadership must be exercised for the welfare of our wives and children rather than for our own pleasure.

2. *Assuming the Role as Senior Partner and High Priest in the Home*

Ephesians 5:23 says, "For the husband is the head of the wife, even as Christ is the head of the church." Also in I

Corinthians 11:3 we read, "But I would have you know . . . the head of the woman is the man. . . ."

These verses do not imply that women are inferior to men, even though men are to be the heads of the homes and the church. In fact, women are in many ways superior to men. This would be a cruel and uncultured world if it were not for the fine attitudes, the good tastes and the refined qualities of women.

Husbands, our responsibility in the home is not as dictators or bosses, but as senior partners. In case of a tie, we may cast the deciding vote!

We as men are to assume the final leadership in the home and the church because God has endowed us for such tasks. While we have innate administrative abilities for such leadership, we do need the counsel and help that women have to contribute, as we make decisions.

Most of all, men are to be the spiritual leaders in the home and to take the initiative in teaching the children the Word of God. We have failed as husbands if we leave it to our wives to assume leadership in spiritual matters with our children. It is God's program for husbands to be the high priests in their homes.

3. *Loving the Wife as Christ Loved the Church*

Over and over the Bible commands the husbands to love their wives. Ephesians 5:25 says, "Husbands, love your wives, even as Christ also loved the church, and gave himself for it." Ephesians 5:28, 29 reads, "So ought men to love their wives as their own bodies. He that loveth his wife loveth himself. For no man ever yet hated his own flesh; but nourisheth and cherisheth it, even as the Lord the church." Colossians 3:19 says, "Husbands, love your wives, and be not bitter against them."

If as husbands we love our wives to this degree, it will

contribute to the making of happy homes. Then unselfishness and a partnership attitude will be a natural thing. We are commanded to love our wives as Christ loved the Church. Christ because of His love labored incessantly for the Church and suffered and died for her. Happy homes are in the making when we husbands have this same unselfish love for our wives.

4. *Providing a Normal Sex Life for the Wife*

It is important to notice that sex was created by God and for a good purpose. It is not evil in itself. Rather, an improper use of it makes it sin.

From the Biblical account of creation, we read that God created mankind male and female, "And God said unto them, Be fruitful, and multiply, and replenish the earth" (Genesis 1:28a). Jesus amplified this when He said, "For this cause shall a man leave father and mother, and shall cleave to his wife: and they twain shall be one flesh" (Matthew 19:5).

These Scriptures say that sexual partnership was made by God for the husband and wife relationship. It was intended for perpetuating the human race and for deepening the love between husband and wife. But when a sexual experience takes place outside of wedlock, it becomes a damning sin. God meant it only for the permanent lifelong union of marriage. God has pronounced judgment upon those who use the sex relationships in other ways.

Sex is a pure and holy thing in the marriage relationship. There is nothing shameful or sinful about it when it functions in the role God ordained for it. The Bible says, "Marriage is honourable in all, and the bed undefiled" (Hebrews 13:4). Again, "Because of prevailing unchastities let every man have his own wife and every woman her own husband. The husband must render to his wife the obligations that are due her, and similarly the wife to the husband. The wife has no exclusive control over her own body, due to the husband, and just so has the husband no exclusive control over his own body, due to the wife.

"Do not deprive each other, except by mutual agreement for a time to devote yourselves unhindered to prayer, and come together again, so that Satan may not tempt you on account of your lack of self-control" (I Corinthians 7:2-5, Berkeley).

This passage tells us that the sex experience is not for procreation alone, but it is a part of marriage that maintains and fulfills love. But this does not give the husband the privilege of using his wife for satisfying his lusts. Sex is to be mutually enjoyed. A wife's feelings, desires and pleasures must be considered.

Selfish indulgence in this area of married life has sown much discord and has been the root of troubles that have often broken up homes. Husbands have a responsibility in exercising restraint and leadership in this area of home life. To fail here is often the cause for an unhappy home.

It is not easy to be a good husband and build a happy home. It takes effort, planning, unselfishness and manliness to fulfill our part of a happy marriage. Again I must remind us that we reap happiness in proportion to our faithfulness in living by God's standards.

V

THE WIFE'S PART

Years ago as a student in college, I took a course in sociology. One class period in that course is still fresh in my memory. The old issue of woman's suffrage was debated. We discussed at length the trend of women leaving their homes and entering into the business, political and entertainment world. Our professor let us air our views for some time, and then he closed the discussion with a stirring speech. This is the essence of it.

He said he was unhappy about modern woman's attempt to compete on man's level. He felt that true gentlemen respected women, looked up to them and considered them as having many higher and finer qualities. To his mind, in competing for man's responsibilities they were lowering themselves and losing the esteem of men. He closed by saying that if women want to come down to our level, then we will treat them as men and they can move their own furniture, carry their own suitcases and open their own doors.

The sociology professor gave us some insights into reasons why, in general, women don't receive the respect and courtesies they once did. But let's go to the Bible and find out God's plan for women in the world. Again I want to emphasize that happy home building demands that each member of the family fill the place that God has planned for him. When one usurps another's position or fails in the duties God has prescribed for him, then unhappiness is being invited into the home.

What are the wife's responsibilities in the home as outlined in the Scriptures? If home life isn't going as it should, perhaps it's the wife's fault. Happiness cannot result in the home if a wife is not fulfilling her God-given duties.

Here are some of the responsibilities of a wife as outlined by God.

1. Regarding the husband as the head of the home.
2. Converting the house into a home.
3. Assuming the responsibilities of motherhood.
4. Providing a normal sex life for the husband.

1. *Regarding the Husband as the Head of the Home*

Ephesians 5:22-24 says, "Wives, submit yourselves unto your own husbands, as unto the Lord. For the husband is the head of the wife, even as Christ is the head of the church: and he is the saviour of the body. Therefore as the church is subject unto Christ, so let the wives be to their own husbands in every thing." Notice this same teaching in I Peter 3:1, 2, "Likewise ye wives, be in subjection to your own husbands; that, if any obey not the word, they also may without the word be won by the conversation [godly living] of the wives; while they behold your chaste conversation coupled with fear." And Ephesians 5:33 says, ". . . and the wife see that she reverence her husband."

These are a few of the Scriptures that teach that a wife is to be subject to the husband. This divine principle is not too popular in our day; there is rebellion against the idea. But that is one of the reasons why there are so many unhappy homes today. When a wife will not live in subjection to her head, she is disobeying God and will suffer the consequences. Someone has said, "A bossy wife is not to be envied, but pitied." She is losing happiness in her unscriptural attitude and spoiling happiness in the home for the family.

Certainly the submission of a wife does not mean slavish subjection, but a joyful working together for a common cause. If the husband loves his wife as Christ loved the church, obedience to him will be glad cooperation. A wife can be happy living in subjection to her husband. John R. Rice says, "It is often insisted upon that in these modern days of liberty and equality no woman could keep her self-respect and live in a home and not be counted equal with her husband in authority. But the same woman who objects to being under the authority of her husband attends clubs of which she is not president. She works in a church of which she is not pastor. She is a citizen of a government where others rule over her. Even the policeman on the corner can command her to stop or go, turn left or right, or may hail her to court where she is as helpless as a child before the law. . . . Men who work for salaries or wages, and women too, must take orders from those in authority. And sensible people can be happy in doing so."[1]

If a wife objects to the headship of her husband, it is an offense similar to a child's disobedience to his parents. Either one is breaking God's law. In the home someone must be the final authority and God has delegated that authority to the husband; the wife is his helper and partner.

2. *Converting the House into a Home*

Modern love quite often pictures the wife as delicate and fragile. She has a life of ease, sleeping late in the morning and spending the afternoons and evenings in social affairs. But this is not God's plan for the wife. Again we go to the Scriptures for instruction on this matter.

[1] John R. Rice, *The Home: Courtship, Marriage, and Children* (eighth printing; Grand Rapids: Zondervan Publishing House, 1957), p. 108.

Titus 2:4, 5 says, ". . . teach the young women to be sober, to love their husbands, to love their children, to be discreet, chaste, keepers at home, good, obedient to their own husbands, that the word of God be not blasphemed." For further instruction we go to that great chapter on the virtuous woman, Proverbs 31. Notice the qualities found in a pure and godly wife. She is not a doll who gives most of her time to clubs and social affairs. "She seeketh wool, and flax, and worketh willingly with her hands. . . . She riseth also while it is yet night, and giveth meat to her household, and a portion to her maidens. . . . She layeth her hands to the spindle, and her hands hold the distaff. She stretcheth out her hand to the poor; yea, she reacheth forth her hands to the needy. She is not afraid of the snow for her household: for all her household are clothed in scarlet [double garments]. . . . She looketh well to the ways of her household, and eateth not the bread of idleness. Her children arise up, and call her blessed; her husband also, and he praiseth her." Wives and mothers like that are the real need of our times.

As a wife you are to love your husband and so live that your husband safely trusts in you. You are responsible for converting your house into a home to which your lover will return each evening. You must do more than cook good meals, keep the house clean and be the mother of his children. You must put your life and love into your work and it must be a delight. This calls for hard work, cheerfulness, songs, flowers, thoughtfulness, careful planning, embraces and kisses. It is taking the ordinary of life and putting love into it so that your lover will anticipate returning to his queen. To practice these principles puts one well on the way in building a happy home.

If a wife nags her husband and is constantly critical of him, she is sowing the seed that will reap an unhappy or broken home. Twice in the Book of Proverbs (21:9 and 25:24) it says, "It is better to dwell in a corner of the housetop, than with a brawling woman in a wide house." And Proverbs 21:19 says, "It is better to dwell in the wilderness, than with a contentious and an angry woman."

It is also important for a wife to keep in mind that if she lacks cheerfulness, fails to keep herself neat and clean, or if she has a dirty and unkept house, she is out of the will of God. These things will contribute to driving a husband from home and set the stage for an unhappy, yes, even a broken home.

I can hear some of you wives say, "Well, if my husband would give me more money, I could dress more attractively and if he would buy a better house, I could make it more inviting."

I am not talking about expensive clothing. I am talking about clean clothing. I am not talking about big houses, expensively furnished, but houses which are kept clean and cheerful which show evidence of originality and loving interest. I have seen some houses with cheap furnishings converted into cozy and attractive homes. Wife, it is your God-given duty to convert your house into a cheerful home filled with love.

3. *Assuming the Responsibilities of Motherhood*

Paul, when he writes to Timothy (I Timothy 5:14), says, "I will therefore that the younger women marry, bear children, guide the house, give none occasion to the adversary to speak reproachfully." The psalmist says that children are blessings from the Lord: "Lo, children are an heritage of the Lord: and the fruit of the womb is his reward" (Psalm 127:3).

Somehow it is popular not to have large families. I suppose having many children is inconvenient and interferes too much with people's social life and many activities. The importance of rearing a family for God has been lost in the lust for other things and selfish pleasures. Society may joke and smile about the big family, but God doesn't. In Psalm 127:5 we learn that big families bring happiness and there is nothing shameful about them.

Wives, it is your ordained responsibility to bear children willingly and rear them in the fear of the Lord. That is a career unexcelled and God has placed the challenge largely in your hands. To bear and rear children cheerfully will help you build happy homes.

4. *Providing a Normal Sex Life for the Husband*

In twenty years of ministerial counsel with thousands of people, I have become convinced that in many unhappy homes the trouble began with an unsatisfactory sex and love life. The failure to provide a satisfying intimate love life either through ignorance or selfishness is one of the largest contributing factors to unhappy and broken homes.

Let me read again this pointed passage of Scripture on the subject, but this time from the Phillips translation, "Nevertheless, because casual liaisons are so prevalent, let every man have his own wife and every woman her own husband. The husband should give his wife what is due to her as his wife, and the wife should be as fair to her husband. The wife has no longer full rights over her own person, but shares them with her husband. In the same way the husband shares his personal rights with his wife. Do not cheat each other of normal sexual intercourse, unless of course you both decide to abstain temporarily to make special opportunity for fasting and prayer. But afterwards you should resume relations as before, or you will expose yourselves to the obvious temptation of the devil" (I Corinthians 7:2-5, Phillips).

In matters of sex, husband and wife need to get information from reliable sources so that ignorance doesn't spoil their happy home and rob them of satisfaction in these intimate experiences provided by God for married people. On the other hand, both husband and wife need to consider the desires and wishes of the other unselfishly. Sex needs to be engaged in with intelligent planning and understanding.

I can't overestimate the importance of having a satisfactory love life for both husband and wife. It is a *must* for building a happy home.

VI

THE CHILDREN'S PART

Chucky, our five-year-old, came running to me the other night as I was working on the lawn. He was excited. "Boy," he said, "I ran a mile tonight."

"Chucky," I inquired, "how do you know you ran a mile?"

He said, "Well, if you run around the track at the college six times, it's a mile. I really got tired, too," he continued, "so I took some of the good short cuts they have."

Many older young people are taking short cuts and still expect to grow up and be happily married, to be good parents, useful citizens, and finally reach heaven. But they, like Chucky, are only fooling themselves. There is no easy way to win happiness, good character and eternal life. Short cuts and compromise always cheat one. The Bible says, "Be not deceived; God is not mocked: for whatsoever a man soweth, that shall he also reap. For he that soweth to his flesh shall of the flesh reap corruption; but he that soweth to the Spirit shall of the Spirit reap life everlasting" (Galatians 6:7, 8).

A father read the following verses in family worship, "Children, the right thing for you to do is to obey your parents as those whom God has set over you. The first commandment to contain a promise was: Honor thy father and thy mother that it may be well with thee, and that thou mayest live long on the earth" (Ephesians 6:1-3, Phillips).

Then he paused saying, "I think this would be a good place for us to stop for a few comments."

At the time, it did not occur to him that the very next verse was an admonition to fathers. He began reading again: "And, ye fathers, provoke not your children to wrath: but bring them up in the nurture and admonition of the Lord" (Ephesians 6:4).

He was continuing his reading when one of the children spoke up with a chuckle and said, "There, Father, I think that would also be a good place to stop for some comments."

In the Ten Commandments that God gave, four have to do with man's duty to God and six with man's duty to his fellow men. We have many human relationships, and so it is striking that one of these six deals with the attitude of children to their parents. This commandment says, "Honour thy father and thy mother: that thy days may be long upon the land which the Lord thy God giveth thee" (Exodus 20:12).

Then, too, the number of times the Word of God refers to this subject and the severe punishment designated for disobedient children reveal the primacy of the matter with God. Here are some Scriptures that tell us how children were to be dealt with if they disobeyed or dishonored their parents in the Old Testament days.

"Withhold not correction from the child: for if thou beatest him with the rod, he shall not die" (Proverbs 12:13).

"He that smiteth his father, or his mother, shall be surely put to death" (Exodus 21:15).

"He that curseth his father, or his mother, shall surely be put to death" (Exodus 21:17).

If young people are disrespectful or disobedient to their parents, the Bible says they are committing a terrible sin. This, like any other sin, needs to be confessed and repented of in order to get forgiveness and peace. It is indeed alarming to note the proportion of parents who are taking orders from their children today, rather than the children obeying their parents.

When the Apostle Paul lists some of the signs of the last days, he includes the sins that result when home life disintegrates. He says, "This know also, that in the last days perilous times shall come. For men shall be lovers of their own selves . . . disobedient to parents, unthankful, unholy, without natural affection" (II Timothy 3:1-3a). The breakdown of parental authority is a sign of spiritual apostasy and of the imminent return of Christ for His Church.

Let's look at the positive side of how children are to treat their parents.

Someone has said that "many a boy at sixteen can't believe that some day he will be as dumb as his dad." It is normal for a young person to feel that he knows a great deal. But young people are commanded to respect the judgment of older people, especially their parents. The Bible says, "My son hear the instruction of thy father, and forsake not the law of thy mother: for they shall be an ornament of grace unto thy head, and chains about thy neck" (Proverbs 1: 8, 9). If for no other reason, a child should honor the instructions and judgment of his parents because the Word of God commands it.

The Bible also commands that children are to obey their parents. It says, "Children, obey your parents in all things: for this is well pleasing unto the Lord" (Colossians 3:20). At another place it says, "Children, obey your parents in the Lord" (Ephesians 6:1).

This does not mean that our parents are always right. They are human and make mistakes, too, but even in those circumstances we are to obey, and God will bless and honor us for our obedience. God rewards for the right spirit and attitude. So we can't lose if we follow the instruction of the Word of God to obey our parents.

The Bible also says to children, "Honour thy father and thy mother, as the Lord thy God hath commanded thee" (Deuteronomy 5:16). Again, "Hearken unto thy father that begat thee, and despise not thy mother when she is old" (Proverbs 23:22). Our parents have sacrificed and worked hard for our best interests. They loved us, provided for us and denied themselves in order to give to us, so we are to honor them.

"It was one bleak morning when Daniel Webster was helping his father build a fence on the rocky New Hampshire farm, that he learned his great ambition was to be fulfilled. He was to go to college!

"His father said to him, 'Son, we intend to wear our old clothes another year. We have put a second mortgage on our farm. I was denied an education for myself, but I am determined that one of my children, anyhow, shall have a chance to be a scholar.'

"That night Daniel did not go to bed, so excited with joy was he. But neither did his father, in the room below. Old and failing, he was turning his back upon a retired life of ease, but took up his work anew with a prayer of thankfulness that his boy was to have a chance in the world.

"It is no wonder, then, that Daniel Webster became one of the most famous men of his day. After he had become great, he humbly said one day, 'The finest gentleman I have ever known, and the most heroic soul, was my father.' "[1]

Children are also to honor their parents by taking care of them when they are old. The Bible says, "Honour widows that are widows indeed. But if any widow have children or nephews, let them learn first to shew piety at home, and to

[1] Herbert Prochnow, *A Treasury of Stories — Illustrations, Epigrams, Quotations* (Boston: W. A. Wilde Co., 1957), pp. 71, 72.

requite their parents: for that is good and acceptable before God" (I Timothy 5:3, 4). And it is in this setting that God says, "But if any provide not for his own, and specially for those of his own house, he hath denied the faith, and is worse than an infidel" (I Timothy 5:8). We are to honor our aged parents by caring for them. God said so.

Young people, in a few short years you will be parents. So treat your father and mother the way that you would like your children to treat you. The Bible is clear – we will reap what we sow. If you are dishonoring, disobedient and disrespectful to your parents, expect to get the same treatment or worse from your children. One can't disobey the Bible and not suffer for it.

In some circles today there is the attitude that if young people sin it is not so serious. The feeling is that God will overlook and excuse youth who disobey the Word of God. But I don't know a single Scripture that says a young person can ignore God's teaching and escape reaping the consequences. Rather it says, "Don't let people look down on you because you are young; see that they look up to you because you are an example to them in your speech and behavior, in your love and faith and sincerity" (I Timothy 4:12, Phillips).

Finally, young people, let's not wait until our parents are dead to respect and honor them. Let's make them happy while they are living – by kindnesses, love and obedience. When one's parents have passed on, one never regrets having honored them while they were living. But one will be sorry if he was mean, unkind and disrespectful to them.

In building happy homes, we must have parents who give their homes and children priority; and the children must respect, honor and obey their parents. To accomplish this, Christ must be the head of our lives and homes.

VII

WHY SOME MARRIAGES FAIL

We are living in an age when we travel faster than sound, broadcast color television, make atomic power, talk by telephone around the world, but we are having great difficulty in building happy marriages. Broken homes are fast becoming the number one social problem.

Some marriages fail because of premarital sinfulness. Frequently happiness for marriage was lost in the "Bay of Courtship" before the "Sea of Matrimony" was reached. Many bring to the marriage altar a life from the basement bargain counter labeled "cheap," damaged and soiled from much handling.

Clarence Macartney has well said, "The laws of God are given for man's good and perfection, and wherever violated they bring their entail of suffering. Prophylactics may save from physical disease; and contraceptives from children; but there is no prophylactic which saves the mind from contamination or the soul from tarnish, and no contraceptive which will prevent the conception of the children of regret, self-despising, and self-degradation."[1]

There are some who believe the devil's lie, that what happens before marriage has no effect upon it. They imagine that getting married is like going from one room into another,

[1] Clarence E. Macartney, "The Way of a Man with a Maid: Adam and Eve," *Christ Life* (n.d.), p. 10.

and closing the door on what is behind. How naive! Rather, it's like taking the wall down between the two rooms.

Every time a person uses sex wrongly, permanent damage is done. It destroys the possibility of belonging wholly to your beloved. The Bible says, "Shun unchastity. All other sin a person commits outside the body, but the unchaste sins against his own body" (I Corinthians 6:18, Berkeley). Premarital sinfulness can be forgiven, but it does not automatically wipe out the damage done.

Immaturity is another cause for broken marriages. One minister hardly thought it necessary to ask the two eighteen-year-olds who had come for marriage the usual question, "Has either of you been married before?" But he asked out of routine. He was shocked when the young man boldly answered, "Yes, sir! We both have. But we are divorced."

Marriage is for adults. Many young people get married before they are grown up. They are neither equipped emotionally nor in experience to make a wise choice of a life companion. Dr. Henry Bowman, who studied divorce for ten years, discovered that in over one-half of all divorces, the couples had married in haste. No mere physical attractiveness or married sex experiences are enough to insure abiding happiness.

Many marriages are broken because the participants were married before they could wisely choose. Dr. James Furboy says, "Studies of divorce and broken marriages all show us that the causes were all present before marriage, and could have been detected."[2]

Many marriages are broken because they were based solely on romantic love. Probably no word has been prostituted and perverted more than love. It has been taken

[2] Dr. James Furboy, Carl Kardatzke, *Happy Marriage Is for You . . . If* (The Warner Press: Anderson, Indiana, 1949), pp. 4, 5.

from its sublime and sacred position in the Bible and has been degraded to pure lust by the sensualists of Hollywood. Several years ago more than ninety per cent of the leading movie stars had been divorced, some five or six times. Hollywood is rightly labeled the divorce capital of the world. The tragedy is that these stars, who emphasize sex and glamor, are the idols of American youth.

Chaplain Wyeth Willard says, "The most subtle enemy of marriage and the home in America today is Hollywood."[3] Leonard Greenway says, "Hollywood stands condemned before God as an industry that has done more to besmirch the sacred tie of marriage than any other agency in the world."

In many of the wildly romantic, gushing, and hectic Hollywood love stories, everything ends up rosy and the "lovers" are ushered into a marital paradise. The young people who have been taught those false concepts of love, try marriage on similar terms and end up with broken homes. If love isn't dealt with properly, it deals with you.

Some marriages don't last because they are entered into as a trial. Some change their mates as they do their cars. When their model begins to age, they are ready to trade for a new one. One counselor for newlyweds said a common question is, "Don't you think that we should wait to have children until we are certain that we are suited to each other?" It's almost as Irvin Cobb has said, "Marriage used to be a contract; now many seem to regard it as a 90-day option." Some people first get married and then get acquainted.

All this shows us how far from God's standards we have gone. Jesus said, "Whosoever putteth away his wife, and marrieth another, committeth adultery: and whosoever marrieth her that is put away from her husband committeth

[3] Wyeth Willard, "The Divorce Evil in American Homes," *The Sunday School Times* (April 30, 1949), p. 387.

adultery" (Luke 16:18). These folks who are making marriage a farce by their divorces and remarriages, are endangering their souls for eternity, according to the Bible.

Others find their marriages have failed because they had wrong motives when they married. Some boys marry girls simply because they are pretty or because of the "frame of the dame." Some girls marry fellows because they are handsome, seem heroic, have good paying jobs, or exciting careers. Some marry to get away from their homes or unpleasant jobs. Others marry because of loneliness or a desire for sex experiences. Some girls will even marry for money. One wife told her husband after the honeymoon that he could be the president, but she would be content with the subordinate position of treasurer.

No marriage will survive, or at least won't be happy, if it is based on any of these superficial reasons. One can't defy the divine purposes of marriage and expect success. God's laws are built into the universe and into our natures, and when we violate them, suffering and disappointment follow.

Many marriages are broken because selfishness or sex ignorance destroyed love. No marriage can succeed if there is a division of devotion or a reservation of affection. This is a cause and effect universe. So when selfishness rules, love begins to die.

Sex is important for married happiness. But like fire, while it is most essential, yet when it gets out of control it can burn one to death and cause great destruction. Sex is basic for marital happiness, but if it is uncontrolled or mismanaged, it can destroy love and break up marriages. Too many husbands and wives use sex on the animal level, rather than in the way God intended, which would cement their marriages.

Many marriages are doomed to failure because God and the Bible were not considered in the forming of the marriage.

You will search the Bible in vain to find one place where happiness in marriage is promised to one who neglects God's principles. Only Christian homes are a guarantee against broken marriages.

A survey of eighteen hundred juvenile delinquents showed that sixty per cent of them came from broken homes. Many of our criminals were born into broken, unhappy or destitute homes. One author says that ninety per cent of our homes are unhappy. So we can expect the fruit of sinning children to come from our unloving and broken marriages.

Naturally a child in an unhappy home will stay away from home. One juvenile court judge said, "If my children lived under the conditions of these youngsters, they too would be coming into court."

If you build your marriage on Jesus Christ, the Rock of Ages, it will stand against the devil's efforts to break it. Marriage is the highest, the most sacred, the most beautiful, and yet the most difficult of human relationships. But when it is entered into in the fear of the Lord, by people who are living for God's glory, it will yield heaven on earth. The Bible says, "Delight thyself also in the Lord; and he shall give thee the desires of thine heart. Commit thy way unto the Lord; trust also in him; and he shall bring it to pass" (Psalm 37:4, 5).

Mark Twain, the American humorist, deeply loved and finally married Olivia Langdon. Twain was not a Christian, but his wife was reared in a Christian home and had pronounced religious convictions. After marriage, because of his love for her, he joined in the family worship and the blessing at mealtime. But Twain couldn't long continue his pretense and finally burst out, "Livy . . . I don't believe in the Bible."

His unbelief gradually had a deadening influence on his wife's spiritual life. Later, in a time of deep sorrow, he tried to encourage her by saying, "Livy, if it comforts you to lean on the Christian faith, do so."

"I can't . . . I haven't any," she replied.

The Bible asks, "Can two walk together, except they be agreed?" How can there be unity in marriage when husband and wife are divided about God? Unity implies agreement. If a marriage is to succeed, the partners must be one in mind, in purpose, in convictions, in faith and in everything that really matters.

When a Christian marries a non-Christian, he disobeys God. The Bible says, "Be ye not unequally yoked together with unbelievers" (II Corinthians 6:14). God cannot bless an unscriptural union. So don't expect your marriage to succeed if you as a Christian deliberately marry an unsaved person. The Bible tells us to marry only in the Lord (I Corinthians 7:39).

One girl, in telling her pastor her plans for marriage, said, "He is not yet a believer in Christ, yet I know the Lord is leading me to marry him." That just couldn't be. God never asks us to disobey Him. Disobedience to God courts disaster.

Never marry to reform your partner, because it seldom works. The peak of your influence on your partner is just before marriage. If he doesn't love you enough to change then, don't be deceived into thinking that it will happen after marriage. Many have had a lifetime of regret because the premarriage promises were never fulfilled.

There are other types of mixed marriages that have difficulty in succeeding, such as those between individuals from very different races, nations or religions. It may not be sin to marry across some of these boundaries, but there are handicaps. Habits, customs, convictions and prejudices are larger hurdles than one thinks. Also in these mixed marriages the children often suffer. In interracial marriages, usually neither race completely accepts the family unit into their fellowship. Inter-faith marriages also create difficult problems for the parents and children.

Your best chance of staying married comes when you are a Christian and marry a Christian and your partner is of your own race, nationality, conviction and faith. Such marriages usually bear the fruit of happiness.

VIII

THE BIBLE SPEAKS ON DIVORCE

The seriousness of marriage can never be overestimated. It has a direct bearing upon future generations through the children. Because of the law of heredity, two people in marriage start a stream of influence, either for good or evil, that may last throughout human history. It even reaches into eternity through the souls of their descendants.

The Scripture tells us that God made marriage for one man and one woman. There was no provision for polygamy. "God made a pair, not a harem." He did not make a male and females or vice versa. A grade school teacher asked one pupil to give his father's name. "Which one?" he replied. "I have had three fathers." What a tragedy! And this is not an isolated case. Is there any wonder that we have so many juvenile delinquents and teen-age criminals? Homes always fail when God's laws are ignored and His teachings spurned. This always courts disaster and regret.

We are shocked and hurt when we hear that thousands of homes have been destroyed by bombs. We need to be shocked and again become sensitive to the many thousands of homes that are wrecked each year by the devil in marital crashes. As Lord Bryce said, "If harm comes to us, it will not be through the strength of bad people but from the indifference of good people." May God give the churches and the lawmakers the fortitude to return to God's Word, the Bible, to find direction and help in these crisis days. No nation can be any purer, stronger or more righteous than its marriages and homes are.

It's amazing how intolerant we are of almost any failure, except the gross failure of mankind's most essential career — marriage, parenthood and homemaking. The people involved need to be warned that they are sinning. God's laws that govern sex, marriage and divorce are holy ground. The moral standards of individuals and nations are tied to divine judgment. God created us and so He has the inherent right to speak authoritatively to us. It is not a question of what we want or like. We must give an account to God. The church and state are held responsible to see that God's decrees are proclaimed. For some decrees we are responsible to see that they are carried out on the earth.

If one out of every four airplanes crashed, the public would demand a thorough investigation. All planes would be grounded; airlines would go out of business; airplane construction companies would go bankrupt and pilots would quit their jobs. No flying would be allowed unless the trouble was found and corrected and more rigid controls begun.

Why is there not a corresponding concern about the many marital crashes? We have one divorce for every four weddings, not to mention the many additional unhappy marriages. We show too little concern for the wrecked homes, separated families, broken hearts, orphaned children and moral delinquency. It's past time that the church and the state demand a thorough investigation. These marital crashes have reached alarming proportions. We need some changed laws and a more serious approach to marriage and divorce. Let's face it — the fate of the family and the fate of civilization go hand in hand. It's a grim tragedy that we have made divorce a sinister joke, rather than the stark disaster that it really is. The Bible says, "If the foundations be destroyed, what can the righteous do?" (Psalm 11:3)

Sometime ago Bill Bryant of Nova Scotia was so engrossed in his hobby that he didn't notice his house was burning down around him. We, too, are so busy with our selfish interests that we don't realize the smouldering fires of unfaithfulness, broken vows and divorce have undermined our homes. Our lack of protest and concern for the bold disobedience to God's laws that govern marriage is allowing this cancer to go unchecked in our sickened civilization.

The past number of years we have freely published information concerning marriage and sex. No detail has been kept back because it was intimate or personal. This was supposed to result in stronger marriages and greater happiness. But the reverse seems to be true. The free and unholy discussion of these things has resulted in more divorces and marital crashes. This sacred subject has been largely discussed from an anti-Christian and anti-moral viewpoint. The Bible says, "Let marriage be held in honor by all" (Hebrews 13:4, Berkeley). When we joke about marriage and sex and defy God's laws governing them, we court disaster. God warns, "Do you not know that . . . neither profligates, nor idolators, nor adulterers, nor partakers in homosexuality . . . shall inherit God's kingdom" (I Corinthians 6: 9, 10, Berkeley).

A drunken man staggered down the sidewalk. Everyone laughed at him except one little boy. It was his daddy, the man whom he longed to be proud of. To him it was not funny.

Broken marriages are a similar evil that for some provide amusing stories. But a broken marriage is sad and sinful, not humorous. Every year millions of homes are broken by desertion, separation and divorce. The stories behind these shattered human relationships are tragic. In this area Satan is winning victories of alarming proportions. The human family is in desperate danger.

Broken homes should concern us all. Their members are filling our penal and mental institutions. Since family life is the foundation of civilization and a divine institution for the good of mankind, the devil is trying to wreck it. Remember, the integrity and strength of any nation depends largely on the happiness and solidarity of its homes.

Loose marriage laws, infidelity and free love are laying an ax to the root of our civilization. Our present practices will corrupt the soul of humanity. The accepted moral standards are simply pouring oil on the flames that are devouring us. We need the courage to go back to the Bible, for only that standard will save us.

Marriage should be entered into as a lifetime contract. One of the tragic sins being committed around the world in our generation is the lightness with which marriage is entered. It has largely lost its sacredness and for many it has no spiritual implications. Marriage, it appears, is often entered into on a trial basis. If it succeeds – good; but if it doesn't the unsuccessful participants will get a divorce and try with someone else. Many homes are broken or unhappy largely because the participants entered marriage without a determined effort to make it a success.

When persons go to the marriage altar with the conviction that divorce is sin and that God ordained marriage for life, then the chances for building a happy home are much increased. But if they believe that divorce and remarriage are permissible, then the chances are also increased for early marital trouble. Often when such is the case, couples are married before they are sure they are in love and before all the lights are green, and psychologically they are not prepared to give their best to their marriage to make it a success. The benefits from tests and trials in married life that could purify and strengthen the marriage ties are not experienced because the partners separate and try again with others.

Harold F. Branch says, "Marriage is a 'job' that people are to see through. They are to look before they leap, and having leaped, they are to stay manfully at the post of duty. There never was a marriage that could not have been a success, nor a marriage that could not have been a failure. No one has a right to happiness who does not win it by devotion, courage, and self-sacrifice. . . . If men and women gird themselves for the adventure of marriage, determined to make a success of the venture at any cost — then they find happiness!"[1]

Divorce has become a popular evil, and it is no longer something that is considered a shame by society. Some newspapers and news magazines announce with a rather jubilant air that this is a woman's fifth husband and a man's sixth wife.

Since divorce is no longer regarded as sin by society and the state, we have an increasing number of divorces and unhappy homes. The seriousness of marriage has been ridiculed. Marriage has largely lost its ability to develop character and maturity because the least little division of opinion is grounds for a divorce. The fact that the Bible calls divorce sin is practically ignored. The percentages of divorce and remarriage go higher almost every year. But don't forget it, we are reaping a harvest of unhappy homes and victimized children. Also there is a rapid increase in juvenile delinquency, and low moral standards in society are corrupting us.

I must raise my voice against this awful sin of divorce and remarriage. God never made a provision for divorce in the whole Bible. It is true that Moses "suffered," that is,

[1] Harold F. Branch, *How to Have a Happy Home* (Chicago: Moody Press, 1926), pp. 7, 8.

"tolerated" some in the Old Testament to write a bill of divorcement. But nowhere do we read that it was justified and not considered sin.

Let's go to God's Word and read for ourselves what it tells us about divorce and remarriage. Jesus tells us in Mark 10:11, 12: "Whosoever shall put away his wife, and marry another, committeth adultery against her. And if a woman shall put away her husband, and be married to another, she committeth adultery." The Apostle Paul says, "For the woman which hath an husband is bound by the law to her husband so long as he liveth; but if the husband be dead, she is loosed from the law of her husband. So then if, while her husband liveth, she be married to another man, she shall be called an adulteress: but if her husband be dead, she is free from that law; so that she is no adulteress, though she be married to another man" (Romans 7:2, 3).

These Scriptures are clear; divorce is sin and remarriage is sin if the former partner is living. And never forget, sin brings reaping! If you want to build a happy home, then enter upon marriage as a serious, spiritual and lifelong responsibility.

Does God ever dissolve a marriage? A divorce is a legal enactment only by the state. When God joins people together in marriage, can a human being dissolve it?

Judge William J. Gaynor, instructing the jury for the famous Powers divorce case said, "If you decide for divorce in this case, remember you only cut the knot tied by the state's law, but you absolutely do not touch the religious or sacramental bond which states that persons are married 'until death us do part' . . . . They are just as much bound by it after we get through with them as they were before. We do not sever it; we do not break it."[2]

[2]William Gaynor, William Evans, *The Right and Wrong in Divorce and Remarriage* (Grand Rapids: Zondervan Publishing House), pp. 16, 17.

Often our laws governing marriage and divorce are not in accord with the Scriptures. But God will judge us by the law of the Gospel and not by the law of the land (Romans 2:16).

Divorce breeds divorce. Our lenient laws have caused a moral laxness that is corrupting us. God has made the marriage bond virtually indissoluble. Let's tell the people; it will be a deterrent to hasty marriages. Married couples would also put more effort into resolving their difficulties.

Divorce is one of the most disillusioning of all human experiences. One aged pastor says, "Divorce in many instances is more of a failure than the marriage which it terminated." We should expect this because divorce militates against God's purpose for marriage. That's why there are no successful divorces; they are only miscarriages of wedded happiness. Divorce is an enemy to the divorcee, the home, the family, the nation and the church. But the devil is constantly trying to legalize it, dignify it, popularize it and promote it.

God ordained marriage for life. God never approved divorce. It was tolerated but never legitimatized.

Let's examine more carefully what Jesus taught about divorce. He says in Matthew 5:31, 32, "It hath been said, Whosover shall put away his wife, let him give her a writing of divorcement: but I say unto you, that whosoever shall put away his wife, saving for the cause of fornication, causeth her to commit adultery: and whosoever shall marry her that is divorced committeth adultery." Here Jesus tells us:

First, the past concessions for divorce are now changed. Jesus said, "It hath been said . . . but I say unto you."

Second, it is sin to put away your mate for any other reason than sexual infidelity. Jesus makes no provision for divorce on the grounds of mental cruelty, incompatibility, drunkenness, insanity or neglect.

Third, if a person divorces for any other reason than sexual infidelity, and then his mate gets immorally involved, he cannot escape part of the blame.

We note in the fourth place that Jesus does not necessarily recommend divorcing an immoral partner; only a permission is given. The burden of New Testament teaching is that one should forgive, restore, or try to reclaim the fallen.

A fifth observation from this Scripture is that anyone who marries a divorced person commits adultery. Jesus says, "Whosoever shall marry her that is divorced committeth adultery."

And in the sixth place we see that an illegitimate divorce does not dissolve the marriage bond. Jesus said one commits adultery if he marries a divorcee. Adultery implies marital infidelity; apparently God considers the first marriage binding.

Many who want to get a divorce go to a spiritual leader they know will approve it. Is this acceptable to God? What a friend, a pastor, a church or a parent says is of lesser authority than the Bible. Jesus said, "He that rejecteth me, and receiveth not my words, hath one that judgeth him: the word that I have spoken, the same shall judge him in the last day" (John 12:48).

Now we go to Matthew 19:3-12 for more of Jesus' teaching about divorce. In this passage the Pharisees came to test Jesus. They asked, "Is it lawful for a man to put away his wife for every cause?" Some spiritual leaders allowed divorce for almost any reason while others had a more strict interpretation. This is also true today.

I am glad these men came to Jesus with this knotty problem of divorce, because He was the best and final authority. Here is how Jesus answered them: "Have ye not read, that he which made them at the beginning made them male and female, and said, For this cause shall a man leave father and mother, and shall cleave to his wife: and they twain shall be one flesh? Wherefore they are no more twain, but one flesh. What therefore God hath joined together, let not man put asunder."

Jesus goes back to the original ordinance of marriage and says it is still in force. And there we have no provision for divorce.

The Pharisees are quick to ask, "Why did Moses then command to give a writing of divorcement?"

Jesus says Moses never commanded divorce, but "because of the hardness of your hearts suffered [or permitted] you to put away your wives: but from the beginning it was not so" (Matthew 19:8). Going on, Jesus says that while Moses tolerated divorce, "I say unto you, Whosoever shall put away his wife, except it be for fornication, and shall marry another, committeth adultery: and whoso marrieth her which is put away doth commit adultery" (Matthew 19:9). Jesus now puts the Old Testament permission for divorce under a ban and establishes the law that is binding upon us. He says that divorce is permitted for sexual infidelity, though it is not encouraged.

When God joins two people in marriage, Jesus says, they are "one flesh," and man is not to put this union asunder. This does seem to imply the possibility of human wickedness sundering the relationship. If it were impossible, there would be no reason to forbid it.

In I Corinthians 7:15 Paul institutes a method to help regulate an illegitimate separation. The Christian partner may not desert the unchristian mate. But if the unchristian mate deserts, the Christian is freed from the marital responsibilities.

Only adultery and desertion are recognized in the New

Testament as legitimate grounds for the innocent party to be freed from his marriage duties. There is more heat than light on the subject of whether adultery and desertion free the innocent party to be remarried. It is clear in the New Testament that divorce is tolerated for only these two reasons. Therefore divorce for any other reason is sin. It is also clear that anyone remarrying on a divorce obtained on other grounds is committing adultery. This is very, very serious because the Bible says the immoral and adulterers will not inherit the Kingdom of God.

Some people try to rule out as uninspired the exceptional clause in Matthew 19:9. This verse clearly allows for divorce on the grounds of sexual infidelity and if remarriage is permitted at all, this verse would be the strongest argument for it. They argue that these few words from Matthew do not fit into the general teaching on divorce and therefore try to throw them out as unscriptural. But I don't think their logic applies here. If I were reporting the speed laws of the State of Virginia, I would give the general laws, such as fifty-five on the open highway and twenty-five and thirty-five in towns and cities. But if I took my driver's examination and the policeman quizzed me on the speed laws, I would give the general laws and the exceptions. To illustrate: I would say that on the highway the speed law is fifty-five, except when going by a school in session, for then the general law doesn't apply and the exception of fifteen miles per hour does.

We know that the general law of God is that marriage is binding until death parts the participants. It is this law that is referred to usually in Scripture. But here when Jesus was quizzed He told of the exception to this general law.

Some people say the innocent party has the privilege to remarry if his partner has deserted him or was guilty of adultery. This is difficult to prove either way. The Bible is your authority and God your judge.

Who is the innocent party anyway? Few ever admit that they are guilty. When one marries hastily, or because of sin marries a wrong partner, or refuses to follow God's leading or parental advice in courtship, how can he be innocent? Some don't find happiness at home because their mate nags, is extravagant, is sexually frigid or extremely selfish. If then because of discouragement or disappointment, they commit adultery, can one say the other party is innocent and free to get a divorce and remarry? The adulterer is certainly not excused or guiltless. But I ask, is the other partner innocent?

Keep it in mind that nowhere in the Bible do we read that separation, or a legal divorce, dissolves a marriage. Neither does adultery as such. The Bible says, "Both honourable marriage and chastity should be honoured by all of you. God himself will judge those who traffic in the bodies of others or defile the relationship of marriage" (Hebrews 13:4, Phillips).

IX

DELINQUENT PARENTS

God's purpose for marriage is to establish homes. After He created them male and female "God blessed them, and God said unto them, Be fruitful, and multiply" (Genesis 1:28). Children fortify marriage. God instituted the marriage unit in order to propagate the race in purity. In other words, children belong in marriage. Marriage is not an end in itself; it is to be a beginning. Two persons become one and then new units of life are to be formed. "Lo, children are an heritage of the Lord: and the fruit of the womb is his reward. As arrows are in the hand of a mighty man; so are children of the youth. Happy is the man that hath his quiver full for them" (Psalm 127:3-5a). The home is the nursery for those who will make up the church and the nation. And the home is the nursery through which each individual passes on his way to heaven or hell.

The family circle is the ideal place for giving moral and religious instruction. Parents are to nurture and teach the commandments of the Lord diligently unto their children. Thus through marriage the responsibility of training and rearing the children is put upon those who were instrumental in bringing them into the world. This binds the family group together in strong vital relationships.

Broken homes are lethal to the welfare of children. One author says, "A boy need not feel ashamed to say his father has died. But to say that his father has left him means to him that his father did not love him." Another authority says, "The place to stop crime is not in the electric chair but in the high chair."

Couples need children, for they more firmly bind the marriage. The Bible says that children are a reward and blessing from God, and happiness results when children are born into the home (Psalm 127:3-5). Ivan Hagedorn says, "The woman who does not want to be bothered with children is a disgrace to her own mother, a fraud to her husband, and a blemish on her own sex, as well as a liability to society."[1]

The Bible tells parents, "Train up a child in the way he should go: and when he is old, he will not depart from it" (Proverbs 22:6). At another place we read, "Fathers, don't overcorrect your children or make it difficult for them to obey the commandment. Bring them up with Christian teaching in Christian discipline" (Ephesians 6:4, Phillips).

These commandments and standards for parents given by God are not being followed. In these matters and others, many have forsaken the Lord and His Word. Consequently juvenile delinquency and crime by adults have grown to shocking proportions. And we can expect it to get worse unless as parents we repent of our sins and return to God and His law. God is still the supreme Potentate whose laws are final, and disobedience to them brings judgment.

Parents, whether we like it or not and whether we accept it or not, the juvenile delinquency problem is a spiritual one. And it is our responsibility as fathers and mothers to teach and train our children in the things of God. But many parents have little or no spiritual concern in their own hearts, so naturally the children get no help from them for their eternal welfare.

[1] Ivan H. Hagedorn, *Seven Blunders in Matrimonial Life* (tract), 1937.

Everywhere these days accusing fingers are being pointed at the parents as the chief cause of juvenile delinquency. There is a growing demand that parents should be held firmly to account for this expanding problem. In other words, many are saying that delinquent parents are our basic problem. Our homes have ceased to function in their God-given role of providing love, discipline and spiritual training.

Someone said recently, "One way to cure juvenile delinquency is to take parents off the streets at night." And that statement is more true than humorous. One night a week at home would be a high average for many a parent these days. In this age of "baby sitters" many parents have forsaken their family responsibilities. Our clubs, social engagements and sporting events have taken priority over our parental duties. As Dr. Robert G. Lee has aptly said, "Our homes are a place where we stay while the automobile is being repaired and when the movie houses are not open."

Dr. Kristen O. Sorheim, Norwegian Minister of Education, says, "America lives mostly outside the home. All night your streets are crowded with cars. You have a profession known as 'baby sitters.' Even in the house, where sometimes you have to be, you aren't living in it but away. You are listening and looking at something else – you have the radio on in one room, the television on in another. You have roofs, yes, and a fairyland of beautiful and useful things under them – everything that money can buy. But not many of you have what we Norwegians would call homes beneath your roofs. Because homes you have to create out of yourselves, and for that you haven't time."

It is certainly a proved fact that "children have their roots in their parents." Therefore when parents are unchristian or absent too much from their homes, they contribute to the delinquency of their children. When we fail to provide the proper discipline, fellowship and spiritual training for our children, we have deprived them of their best defense against evil. It is in these areas that many parents have betrayed their children and have robbed them of protection from the wicked world.

The great tragedy is that many parents are not working at the root of the problem. We can provide better schools, more recreational facilities, and give our children higher standards of living, but this is not getting to the real problem. We can also make more laws, provide more policemen and build more jails and houses of correction, but we are still not dealing with the problem at its source. Many of our juvenile delinquents are not living in squalor. They come from our better homes. Police Chief William H. Park of Los Angeles says, "It is the over-privileged child who is causing the most trouble today. He has been given so much in the way of material things that he is going haywire looking for new satisfactions."

Our children need help from God. They don't have the power or ability in themselves to overcome the devil and his temptations. They are victims of a depraved nature and an evil world, and unless we help our children spiritually, we are not providing them with permanent help.

Education and high standards of living have not solved our sin and crime problems. Our standards of living are probably the highest in world history and our schools and recreational centers have never been better, but almost every year we break new records in crime. We also know that many of these crimes are being committed by clever and educated people. Some of those who head crime syndicates in our world are educated geniuses and they are people with high standards of living, materially. Evil and wickedness are not confined to those who live across the tracks, as we all know.

What more proof do we need? We cannot solve our sin

problem without God and His laws. It's the age-old situation of self-sufficient man thinking he can run his own program and he doesn't want God meddling. When will we learn? When will we humble ourselves and take God's remedy? We have abundant evidence and proof that the Bible works, but we are too proud to repent of our sins and to ask God for His mercy and help. We have been going our own way, but not without suffering the consequences. Our sinful sowing has brought us misery and trouble unending.

Any careful student of world history will attest the truth of this statement from the Bible, "Righteousness exalteth a nation: but sin is a reproach to any people" (Proverbs 14:34). One doesn't have to look beyond his own community to see that godliness pays big dividends and sin lets one down. It is not the sincere followers of Christ who degrade their communities and defame their nations. Those things are being done by those who neglect and reject God's laws.

Several years ago Judge Sam Davis Tatum of the Juvenile Domestic Relations Court of Nashville, Tennessee, wrote: "The Juvenile Court over which I preside has jurisdiction over children under seventeen years of age, who have violated the law. Since June 1, 1939, I have tried approximately 4,800 cases. Of this number only twenty-nine have a regular Sunday school or church record." Please tell me why such statements are not convincing proofs to parents of the value of spiritual training. Yet in spite of such overwhelming evidence, parents still neglect the spiritual life of their children. In their selfish pursuits and with their own depraved hearts, they care little or nothing about God's laws and the spiritual responsibilities He has given them as parents.

One judge in juvenile court said recently, "So far, I have not had a child in juvenile court whose father or mother attended either Sunday school or church regularly." This is another testimony of the vital part and responsibility parents have in the juvenile delinquency problem. We cannot escape it as parents – one of the major causes of juvenile delinquency is the breakdown of our homes, particularly in the area of spiritual responsibility.

As parents we have become more interested in money, pleasure and sin than we are in the Bible, the church and God. Let's never forget it, a child's religion starts with his parents. A child's sense of values, his ethical and moral standards and his general outlook in life are largely absorbed from the example his parents have set before him. We have let our children down. We have failed them in the place that counts most, in their spiritual and eternal welfare.

We haven't taken time to teach our children the Bible, or to take them to church, or to pray with them. Rather we have turned over our parental responsibilities to other agencies, such as the school, the clubs and the Sunday school, and we are spending our energies in getting money and the things it can buy. We don't want our children and their training to interfere with our work, our parties, other social engagements and pleasures. Whether we accept it or not, juvenile delinquency is largely the outgrowth of adult delinquency.

David D. Allen says, "There are thousands of parents who have given their children everything but God. They have provided them with nourishing food, warm clothing, and liberal educations . . . but no Saviour. They have showered them with gifts and protected them from harm . . . but have not provided a family altar.

"They have read to them Dick Tracy and Superman, but

not the Bible. They have taken them to the movies, but not to Sunday school. They have cursed before their children, but never prayed. Thus thousands of children have lived to curse their parents for bringing them into the world and raising them without Christ."[2]

I can hear some of you parents protest and say, "Our children have more advantages than any former generation on earth." You say, "Why, we have given them schools, public parks, organized clubs, and have built all kinds of places for recreation and entertainment. Our young people have more books, magazines, games, radio and television programs to keep them occupied than ever before."

In addition to the thousands of youth centers we have given them, we now have trained sociologists, psychologists, psychiatrists and criminologists to help our children. Also recreational and youth leaders have been trained and provided. You ask, "What more can we do? We have provided well for our children."

These things are all true and we haven't nearly exhausted the list of helps and advantages our children and young people have that former generations never knew. But the fact still remains, juvenile delinquency is increasing and juvenile crimes are becoming more serious and terrible. Someone has said that many teenagers have their own three "R's" these days – raid, 'reck and ruin.

One of the contributing factors of juvenile delinquency is that we have confused our young people. When the Bible is forsaken, we have no final authority. The children may be taught one thing at home and another at school, another at church, and another over radio and TV – all of which frustrate and confuse them.

[2] David D. Allen, *I Accuse My Parents* (Tract Club of America, n.d.).

As adults we need to repent and return to God's unchanging Word. In the Bible we have God's moral law and the standard by which the world will be judged. Let us remember that the Bible speaks of "the day when God shall judge the secrets of men by Jesus Christ according to my gospel" (Romans 2:16).

X

IMPORTANCE OF FAMILY LIFE

Several years ago our local newspaper gave us the account of two young men being executed before a double firing squad. This was their reaping for having killed a man during a service station robbery.

The day before they were executed they issued a statement in which they blamed their situation on lack of "a fair chance in life."

Their statement said, "Coming from broken homes we grew up in neglect. May our tragic lives and ending serve as a warning to all—young and old."

These young men rightly said that while they committed the crime, the blame must be shared by their parents. Their parental home had failed first, and their tragic lives were largely the fruit of that failure. The family is the basic structure of civilization. So when the home fails, there is a moral breakdown.

The Lord made abundant provision so that we can build happy homes. Our best interest is His first interest. His services can be had without money, and they are available to everyone. Jesus said, "Seek ye first the kingdom of God, and his righteousness; and all these things shall be added unto you" (Matthew 6:33).

Elton and Pauline Trueblood point up, in a book they have written, some trends in our home life that are shocking. They say, "In spite of the different labels, we are more like the Russians than we realize or choose to admit. In no area of our experience is the developing similarity more disturbing than that of family life. . . . We are doing by neglect much that the Marxists have done by social planning."[1]

They have the philosophy that the home exists for the state. It simply becomes a tool in the government's hands. In whatever way the family can serve the state, it is used, regardless of what happens to the family unit as such.

We, of course, in our Christian-oriented culture and background revolt at this. To us the family and home are sacred and important. We believe that our homes exist in their own right and are fundamental to civilization. It has been proved that strong homes develop good character, make pleasant communities and build strong nations. But our home and family life is deteriorating in the presence of materialism, pleasure, selfishness and sin.

Let me point out four things that Communism is doing to dissolve the family. And sad to say, we are automatically without intent arriving at the same place.

Communism, in the first place, has deliberately undermined the dignity of the home. Communists say that its only reason for existing is to benefit the state. So every practice of home and family life that interferes with the state is ruled out. Godless leaders argue that home life, as we know it, is largely because of Christian influence and is used to promote God and His program. They reject God and deify the state. So they believe they have the right to alter family life to serve their program, just as they say we have done in the past.

We, of course, criticize this philosophy, but unconsciously many of us are going the same direction. The only difference is that we let business, pleasure and social affairs

[1] Elton and Pauline Trueblood, *The Recovery of Family Life* (New York: Harper and Bros., 1953), p. 13.

become the gods that get priority over our home and family life. In many homes the family no longer comes first. And in some it doesn't even come second or third. Norman Harrison says, "In an appalling number of cases these houses are merely places where people exist – where they eat, sleep, argue and feel bored, perhaps, but they are not homes. Many persons lodge at home, but they live elsewhere, in the multiplicity of interests on the outside, finding their friends, their pleasures, their chief achievements apart from the home ties."[2]

Several years ago I read about a real estate salesman who tried to sell a house to a newly married couple. The wife said, "Why buy a home? I was born in a hospital, reared in a boarding school, educated in a college, courted in an automobile, and married in a church. I get my meals at a cafeteria, live in an apartment, spend my mornings playing golf and my afternoons playing bridge; in the evenings we dance or go to the movies; when I am sick I go to the hospital; and when I die I shall be buried from an undertaker's. All we need is a garage with a bedroom."

I realize this is exaggerated, but for many people it gets too close to describing the way they live. Many children are growing up in homes that are little more than boarding houses with a lunch counter. Then we wonder why children get into crime and wickedness. We can expect juvenile delinquency to increase unless we parents make our homes places of love and security. Yes, we must do even more; our homes must be headquarters for spiritual training for our children.

The Bible commands parents to teach and train their children. We are guilty of sin before God and we rob our

[2] Norman B. Harrison, *Hallowing the Home* (Wheaton: Van Kampen Press, 1950), p. 7.

children of basic help for time and eternity when we neglect to provide good spiritual homes for them.

The real centers of interest in many families lie outside their homes. This is true for parents and children. For example if we can make a few extra dollars on another job, we take it even though it means uprooting the family and requires living in temporary or inadequate quarters. This robs the children and family of some of the most important character builders. They lose the community "belonging" feeling. They must adjust to new schools, churches, friends and situations, all of which often turn out to be handicaps to strong family life.

I need not recount the many other practices in our modern and industrial age that are disintegrating our home life. Our families are losing their importance and dignity in our fast, modern culture.

In the second place, Communism decentralizes the home so that the nation can double its labor power. Both sexes work side by side. The women have left their job of being mothers and homemakers and have become tools for the state.

Here again we are following suit. We have lost our vision of what the home and family ought to be. More and more women are working and living outside the home. The Bible says, "I will therefore that the younger women marry, bear children, guide the house, give none occasion to the adversary to speak reproachfully" (I Timothy 5:14). Again it says young women are "to be sober, to love their husbands, to love their children, to be discreet, chaste, keepers at home, good, obedient to their own husbands, that the word of God be not blasphemed" (Titus 2:4, 5).

William Ward Ayer says, "You cannot justify . . . the unspeakable and irretrievable damage done to the nation by emptying the home of its mothers for work in factories and turning their children loose to run the streets in sodden loneliness or participating in petty crimes."

Many wives go to work and the birth of children is delayed until a beautiful house is built or money accumulated. Usually in time the standard of living that is adopted necessitates the wife's continued working to help pay the bills. So we are arriving at the same place as Communism in that our homes are being decentralized. The only difference is that while they adjust the home and family to serve the state, many of us do it to serve the gods of selfish desire, things and pleasure.

This brings us to our third point. In order for Communism to use mothers in competitive work, the idea has been promoted that the state can educate the children as well or better than the home. So they provide nurseries for the little tots and ways to teach and take care of the older children while the mothers work.

Is this too different from conditions in our western world? The center of a child's education used to be the home. This is no longer true in most cases. Many mothers have left the home except to eat and sleep. We, too, put the children in nurseries and provide methods to care for the older children while mother works. And often dad and mother rush home from work, eat a bite, hire a baby sitter, and rush off for some evening social engagement or sports event.

And to a great extent we have turned over the education of our children to the schools, churches, camps, community, radio, television and movies. So our family unit has become a rather meaningless thing. Our selfish interests, high material standards and social engagements take priority over our homes and family life. Often we console ourselves by providing material things for our children, which usually just spoil them more. We seldom give our children ourselves, their parents, which they need most. By neglect, many are robbing the nation of its strongest asset, good Christian homes.

Finally, Communists, in order to minimize the home and family, had to take a low view on sex. They, of course, reject the Bible and are atheists, and so immorality is not considered sinful. To them sex is for pleasure and for propagating the race. It's a personal matter and not considered sacred.

But are sex and the home sacred to us? Many pagan countries have a higher view of the marriage ties than we have. Our emphasis on sex and pleasure has undermined our high moral standards. For many people in our area of the world, sex is also considered an amoral matter. By our materialistic and social emphasis, we have lost the Biblical concept of sin.

The Bible is clear that a wrong use of sex will bring judgment and damnation. It says, "Marriage is honourable in all, and the bed undefiled: but whoremongers and adulterers God will judge" (Hebrews 13:4). Let us repent and live to make our homes and families strong fortresses for Christ and the Church. The only alternative is the loss of the things we cherish most.

A father told his little boy about the lamb that found a hole in the fence and crawled through. It wandered far away. A wolf was trailing the lamb but the shepherd rescued it just in time.

When the story was over the little boy asked his father, "Did they nail up the hole in the fence?"

Let's repair the fences in our homes and families through which many of our children are going astray. To do this we must go back to the Bible and adopt its standards for home and family life. This is the only way to build a happy home and save our children.

XI

CHILDREN NEED TO BE REARED

Johnny went fishing. His parents thought he was in school. On his way home he met one of his school chums. Seeing that he had a fishing line, the chum asked, "Catch anything?"

"No," replied Johnny, "I haven't been home yet."

An important factor in helping children with behavior problems is to start early, before the problems become acute. The old sayings, "An ounce of prevention is worth a pound of cure," or "A switch in time saves nine," are applicable. Therefore, when our homes are ungodly and unhappy, our children miss one of their greatest protections against their becoming delinquents. God says, "Train up a child in the way he should go: and when he is old, he will not depart from it" (Proverbs 22:6).

I read recently about a boy who was punished by his mother for a misdeed. "You should turn a deaf ear to temptation," she scolded.

In tears, the boy protested to her, "But Mommy, I don't have a deaf ear."

The boy was right, none of us has a deaf ear to temptation. For every one of us sin has a natural pull and is a temptation to our human natures. One must go against the gravity of his flesh to live a clean life. The Bible reminds us over and over that no one can finally overcome this pressure of temptation without God's help.

The Scriptures make it clear that man naturally is a victim of his own evil desires, in one way or another. In fact, that is why Jesus came into our wicked world to become our Saviour. God knew that we were doomed to our own evil appetites unless He provided a remedy. He did this in the person of His Son, Jesus Christ.

The Bible tells us that "all we like sheep have gone astray," and that none of us is righteous, no not one. We have "all sinned and come short of the glory of God." But out of love and mercy God provided a Saviour to redeem us. However, this provision only applies to those who of their own free will accept it. Parents are to help their children understand their need of Christ and to encourage them to become Christians. Some parents are more concerned about a sick animal or a loss in their business than they are about their delinquent or disobedient children. Our material emphasis and lack in spiritual desire are dead giveaways of what our greatest concerns are. As long as this continues, we can expect our children to live in sin. There are no bypasses around God's laws of sowing and reaping in kind.

There are today many old, gray-headed parents sitting in their living rooms weeping. Their hearts are broken because their children have grown up and have disgraced the family and have caused unending trouble. Some of these children are behind bars. The thing that is so crushing to the parents is that they failed to give their children a spiritual heritage, the thing they needed most. Now they see their mistake, but their sin of spiritual neglect is now in the reaping stage.

The late George W. Truett tells an experience he had one Sunday morning after preaching on the theme, "No man liveth unto himself."

An old man who had wept all through the sermon told his pastor this tragic story after the service. He said, "I am the sad proof of the tragedy of a wasted influence.

I came at sixty-eight to Christ, and as I came to this church house this morning, I came by the homes of my three sons, and I begged each one of these sons to come to church with me, and they all shrugged their shoulders and said, 'We guess, Father, that we will start going to church when we get to be about sixty-eight.' Then I tried their sons, some of them coming into young manhood, my dear grandchildren, and they looked at one another with a wink, and said, 'Grandpa, we guess we will start going to church when we are about sixty-eight or seventy.' "

The old man continued, "I came on without child or grandchild. I am myself, sir, the awful proof of the tragedy of a wasted influence." Then he stood and looked at the pastor with a pathos he would never forget, stretched out one of his strong arms and said, "I would have that arm severed from my shoulder if I could turn time backward and live my life over again – if I could undo my wasted influence." And then, with a sob never to be forgotten, he said, "Sir, I would be willing to have my head severed from my body, if I could go back and teach my little boys by example how a Christian father ought to live."[1]

This is not a rare experience. It is all too common. We can give our children no greater heritage than an example of holy living and faithful Christian training.

Another reason why some children are disappointments is that many parents have forsaken God's methods of child training. The wise in this world have declared the Bible out of date and no longer practical in many of its teachings. One example is in the area of discipline for children. They now tell us that children are no longer to be punished for their misdeeds. Rather, children are to have their own way so that their personality, individuality and self-expression

[1] George W. Truett, *A Quest for Souls* (Nashville: Broadman Press, 1917), p. 98.

are not hindered. Consequently the tide has turned and now in many homes parents obey their children instead of following the Scriptural pattern that children are to obey their parents.

Someone said recently that "a sound that is rapidly disappearing from the home is that of the parental foot being put down." It is past time that we return to God's Word and let it become our rule book of life. God's way is still the best. The Bible is not out of date in its child training methods. Our departure from them has only brought heartache and trouble.

God says parents, not juvenile courts, are to discipline their children. But since fathers and mothers have failed to discipline their youngsters, the law must. Someone has said that everything in our modern homes is controlled by a switch except the children. We would have less heartache over our children if we controlled them more by the switch and had fewer of the luxuries that are switch controlled.

Discipline is an important factor in building a happy home. These are serious times when many parents have so lost the respect and confidence of their children that good discipline can't be administered. Some parents are so busy that they don't know what their children do or where they go. Naturally they have little control over them. Others have adopted the modern psychological approach. Their children are permitted to have their own way for fear it might scar their personalities. One prominent psychologist and criminologist has said, "We have been so afraid that punishment makes neurotics that we are now burdened with a new crop of psychotics unable to relate themselves even to the minimum orderliness of the world." The Bible says, "Foolishness is bound in the heart of a child; but the rod of correction shall drive it far from him" (Proverbs 22:15).

The Scriptures are clear that punishment and discipline are essential for developing character in the children. They say, "Chasten thy son while there is hope, and let not thy soul spare for his crying" (Proverbs 19:18).

Some parents feel they can't correct and punish their children because they love them, but the Bible says we hate our children if we won't punish them. Love would punish the child so that he doesn't continue in his wayward course. Proverbs 13:24 says, "He that spareth his rod hateth his son: but he that loveth him chasteneth him."

Certainly we are not contending for brutality. Neither should we punish in anger. I realize that some parents are too severe in their punishments. But the modern trend of not using the rod of correction at all is unbiblical. The Bible says, "The rod and reproof give wisdom: but a child left to himself bringeth his mother to shame."

The truth of this verse has testimonies in every community. Parents, if you want to be brought to shame, then let your children go unpunished for their misdeeds. The Bible says, "Withhold not correction from the child: for if thou beatest him with the rod, he shall not die. Thou shalt beat him with the rod, and shalt deliver his soul from hell" (Proverbs 23:13, 14).

We have all heard the old saying, "Spare the rod and spoil the child." That is Bible philosophy. I am convinced that many parents would have avoided some of their troubles with their children if they had had more "board meetings" several years earlier. Someone has well said, "Too many parents are not on spanking terms with their children."

There are many ways to discipline and punish a child apart from the rod. In some cases and with some children other forms often accomplish the most. To deny a child that which he enjoys most or to take away his privileges often disciplines the most effectively. The important thing is to correct and teach the child. Parents continually need to resort to God in prayer to find which method of discipline will be the most effective. But when we neglect to discipline and punish our disobedient children, we sin by God's law. This sin of omission by parents will not go unpunished by God.

A striking illustration of God's attitude toward delinquent parents in child discipline is seen in the Old Testament high priest Eli. God told Samuel, "In that day I will perform against Eli . . . For I have told him that I will judge his house for ever for the iniquity which he knoweth; because his sons made themselves vile, and he restrained them not. And therefore I have sworn unto the house of Eli, that the iniquity of Eli's house shall not be purged with sacrifice nor offering for ever" (I Samuel 3:12-14).

Eli knew about his sons' misdeeds, but he didn't punish or restrain them, and God brought judgment upon him. Father and mother, are you guilty of the sin of omission by neglecting to teach and discipline your children? If you are, remember God will punish for this sin also.

Several years ago J. Edgar Hoover wrote, "More and more children are being sacrificed upon the altar of indifference as parents throw aside responsibility. Selfishness is the keynote of the day and materialism the inspiration for living. God in many instances is not accepted in the home and concepts of morality have been relegated to the junk heap."[2]

Mr. Hoover, head of our FBI for many years, points up in this statement that our greatest family deficiency today is that parents have lost the meaning of what a home ought

[2] Nelson Veltman, *Save Our Homes* (Back to God Sermon, 1956), pp. 34, 35.

to be. Our failure is not only in living below the standard but in not even knowing what the standard is.

The late William Ridgway tells about a young man he met one evening years ago. The stranger was a wire rope salesman and was excited because he was going home. He had not yet seen their first baby, who had been born since he left on his business trip.

Mr. Ridgway said, "Roebling, if an angel, all in white with silver wings, should come gliding down upon that golden moonbeam, and balancing herself upon the porch rail should say, 'I'll make that new baby boy of yours just the sort of man you would like him to be,' say, Roebling, what would you ask the angel to make him?"

After a long period of silence the wire rope man said: "You take me on the short lock. I never thought of that before. I don't know what I should ask for the boy to be."

"Would you say, 'Make him a wealthy man'?"

"No, indeed."

"A famous scholar?"

"No."

"Smart and shrewd?"

"No, sir."

"Great in politics?"

"Not on your life."

"Social lion?"

"No."

"Hustling business man?"

"N-o-o-o, no, I don't believe I would, if I only have this one chance. I happen to know some 'hustling business men.' I try to sell to them. Some are not so 'desirable.'"

"Well, what would you like to have that boy grow up to be?"

"As I told you before, I'm stumped for an answer. I just don't know."[3]

This man, like many others, was starting a family without a clear knowledge of his responsibility. How can we steer our children toward ideals and goals if we don't have them in our planning or in our living?

[3] William H. Ridgway, *The Christian Gentleman* (Boston: W. A. Wilde Co., 1937), pp. 13, 14.

XII

THE INFLUENCE OF THE HOME

Many parents are unhappy because their children have grown up and have made a mess of their lives, and have disgraced the family. Some have become involved with the law, some are living deeply in sin, and still others have had unhappy marriages. This has happened largely because parents failed to put first things first when the children were growing up.

George Washington in his farewell address declared, "Let us not indulge the supposition that morality can be maintained without religion. Regardless of the influence of refined education on minds of particular structure, reason and experience forbids us to expect that national morality can long endure an exclusion of religious principle."[1]

Too many parents have tried to train their children by their words but have failed to be an example to them. When children are small, their parents are the people they admire most. So example is a powerful influence. This is why one lad said to his mother, "Dad never goes to Sunday school and church and as soon as I'm big enough I'm not going either!"

Our children are not stupid. If they see that mother never misses her club meetings, but lets the least little thing keep her home from church, they know which she feels is the most important. And dad religiously attends the lodge meet-

[1] Nelson Veltman, *Save Our Homes* (Back to God Sermon, 1956), p. 33.

ings and never fails to keep his golf engagements, but he only gets to church on Easter and for the Christmas play. Say, if you were a child and admired your dad, what would you think of church?

> No driving rain will keep us away,
> When we have tickets to the play;
> But let one drop the pavement smirch
> And it's too wet to go to church.

I was visiting in a home several years ago when my host asked if I was a descendant of Barbara Hostetler. He said he had a book that had the names of all her direct married descendants for over one hundred years. I told him we don't have an "l" in our name, but likely we stem from the same family trunk; someone probably changed the spelling of the name a little somewhere along the line.

The book traced the direct married descendants of this Ohio couple for over one hundred fifty years. It did not count those who died in youth or those who grew up but were never married. Think of it, in 156 years there were more than 15,550 direct descendants of one married couple – Barbara Hostetler and her husband.

Some people are cocky and resent anyone's suggesting how they should live. If society or the church recommends that they make some changes, they proudly announce, "I am my own boss and shall live just as I please. I don't need any suggestions from anyone. If I want to get drunk, I'll get drunk; if I want to gamble, I'll gamble; if I want to curse, I'll curse; and if I want to go to church, I'll go to church. It's the business of no one else."

That is right in a sense. A person can live the way he wants to, but in another sense he can't. What we are and how we live affects those with whom we associate. Our children most of all are affected by our lives.

If Barbara Hostetler and her husband had lived careless and wicked lives, then the history of their 15,550 descendants would have been one story. But if they were Christian parents, who regularly attended church, studied their Bibles, had family worship, and lived godly lives, then the history of their 15,550 descendants is another story. What a father and a mother are determines, to a large extent, what their descendants will be. If you are a father or a mother, keep it in mind that your children will most likely follow in your steps. A good illustration of this is found in II Timothy 1:5. The Apostle Paul explains in part at least why Timothy was a spiritual giant. He says, "I call to remembrance the unfeigned faith that is in thee, which dwelt first in thy grandmother Lois, and thy mother Eunice; and I am persuaded that in thee also."

It is a blessed and wonderful privilege to have children, but a tremendous responsibility. The wise man, Solomon, tells us, "Train up a child in the way he should go: and when he is old, he will not depart from it" (Proverbs 22:6). What we learn in childhood stays with us all through life. We are aware that the teaching and the training we received in early youth is still with us. It always will be. When a person is young, his mind and heart are plastic, easy to mold and influence. Often in those years a person's destiny in time and eternity is set.

Clarence Benson in his fine book entitled, *An Introduction to Child Study*, says, "At no time are the senses as keen or the memory as clear as during the child life. A child of six has just as quick perception as a man, and the memory powers of ten will never be surpassed. At no time are there as many criminals made or converts won as during the adolescent age. The adult life, while distinct from the child life and the adolescent life, is wholly built upon the foundation of this early period." Father and mother, you can live the way you wish, but don't forget, the character you have and the teaching and environment you give your children will to a large extent determine the kind of men and women your children will become. That in turn will influence greatly the kind of grandchildren and later descendants you will have. To build a happy home you must live godly lives and teach your children in the fear and admonition of the Lord.

What we give our children in childhood will never leave them—be that good or evil. Remember that as parents we are responsible to God for what our children learn and from whom they learn. It is under our direct teaching or within our control that our children receive ideas and develop in ways that will stay with them until they die. That which is implanted in youth is generally there for life.

MOLDING IN CLAY

I took a piece of plastic clay
And idly fashioned it one day;
And as my fingers pressed it still,
It moved and yielded to my will.

I came again when days were past;
The bit of clay was hard at last;
The form I gave it, it still bore,
But I could change that form no more.

I took a piece of living clay
And gently formed it day by day,
And molded with my power and art
A young child's soft and yielding heart.

I came again when years were gone;
It was a man I looked upon;
He still that early impress wore,
And I could change him never more.

—Author Unknown

Certainly you must have discovered that the old people forget about yesterday and the recent past, but the experiences and the training of their childhood are still fresh and vivid. In fact their conversations are mostly about those things. They can retell incidents in detail that happened during their childhood. They can still quote perfectly Bible verses or poems they learned early in their youth. They still sing the songs and hymns learned at home or at church when a child. All this verifies the Scripture that says what we teach our children and build into their character is there for their lifetime. If we teach them the Bible and about Christ, they will never lose that teaching. If we don't, likely our children will never become Christians. What we teach our children is not the final determining factor in their eternal destiny, but it is perhaps the strongest influence they will ever have toward heaven or hell. Mother and Dad, in which direction are your lives and influence leading your children?

One time I worked with a man who seldom attended church. When I spoke to him about it, he said that he was too busy with his business; but he hurried on to say, "I make my children go to Sunday school every Sunday."

I asked him, "How long will your children attend Sunday school if you don't go with them? They will attend until they are about thirteen or fourteen and then try to get them to go if you don't go yourself!" The man has reaped bitter experiences in the family since then. How often we have seen this in many families! Are you sending your children to Sunday school and church, or are you going with them? You will reap heartaches some day if you are simply sending your children to Sunday school and church and not accompanying them.

If you want to build a happy home, you will need to follow God's program for parents. The Bible says, "Ye fathers, provoke not your children to wrath: but bring them up in the nurture and admonition of the Lord" (Ephesians 6:4). And I am impressed when I read again the address that Moses gave to the Children of Israel after forty years of leadership. He said, "Hear, O Israel: The Lord our God is one Lord: and thou shalt love the Lord thy God with all thine heart, and with all thy soul, and with all thy might. And these words, which I command thee this day, shall be in thine heart: and thou shalt teach them diligently unto thy children, and shalt talk of them when thou sittest in thine house, and when thou walkest by the way, and when thou liest down, and when thou risest up" (Deuteronomy 6: 4-7).

Did you notice that Moses said parents were first to love God and to have His commandments in their hearts? Then they were to teach their children diligently what they had experienced. Likely we can teach our children little that we as their parents don't possess or practice. So with many parents being in spiritual poverty, we can't expect the children to have spiritual concerns and Biblical standards. How could children have higher ideals and concerns than their father and mother whom they idolize?

Parents, we have a serious role to fill. It's not a marginal task either. The implications are tremendous. We have the largest and the strongest influence on our children. Their convictions, character and ideals are mostly formed by what we are. This is what is implied when the Bible says, "The Lord is longsuffering, and of great mercy, forgiving iniquity and transgression, and by no means clearing the guilty, visiting the iniquity of the fathers upon the children unto the third and fourth generation" (Numbers 14:18). In other words, our trail of influence reaches down into the next generations through our children. Remember, our children are largely "chips-off-the-old-blocks." So we as parents have an important stake in the eternal destinies of our children and grandchildren.

We cannot effectively teach righteousness to our children unless we are righteous. Let us not deceive ourselves into thinking that we can teach our little folks something we don't possess. What we are speaks so loudly they won't hear what we say. Our teaching and training will go in one ear and out the other unless we are examples of what we teach.

Parenthood is one of the most sobering and far-reaching responsibilities a person will ever have. Our children firmly believe in us and imitate us; thus what we are molds the personalities and characters of our children.

I still remember how I regarded my father when I was a little boy playing with my playmates. I thought I had the best dad in the world. What my dad did or said was exactly right, and if any of my playmates said his dad was better than mine, he had better run, because that was a statement that needed to be corrected. My dad's words and deeds were by far superior to any other's. He was my hero, practically my god, and girls consider their mothers the same way at this age.

Almost without exception in every boy's life his father, for a period of time at least, is his ideal and the mother is that for the girls. I think one of the greatest tragedies that can come into a child's life is discovering that his parents are not what he thought they were. When a father ceases to be the hero of his boys and the mother ceases to be the heroine of her girls, a tragic blow has been dealt their children. In a child's mind the people most like God and Jesus are his parents. Woe to those parents who wilfully betray that superb confidence and trust. It will damage seriously the character of a child.

Parents, if we want to build happy homes that will last,

we must be vital Christians. Much is at stake in being a father or a mother. I tremble when I see what ungodly lives some parents are living. What will their children and grandchildren be like? Only days of unhappiness and regret lie ahead for them. We can see a rapid growth in juvenile delinquency, defiant attitudes and disrespect for authority in many of our youth. Are these not the results of the failure of parents?

If the world stands, likely in a hundred years from now you will have thousands of descendants. What they will be like will be partly determined by what you are and how you rear your family. Life is serious. I plead with you if you have not, to become Christians and to put Christ in the center of your home.

A superintendent of schools said, "The crime wave must be broken on the hearthstone." And a high school principal said, "If young people are on the right track, they were put there in the home." More and more our leaders are telling us of the importance of home and family life. And more and more our officers of the law are telling us that the increase of crime is due to the disintegration of the home and family. Many are neglecting their parental duties in order to live in a beautiful house, and they end up with the house but have lost their chances to have a beautiful home and a happy family.

I urge you to repent if you are neglecting your parental duties. Remember, only when Christ is the head of your family are you guaranteed a happy home.

Someone wrote this beautiful prayer. If each of us would pray it sincerely and live its sentiments, it would change the destiny of nations and would go a long way in preparing our children for heaven.

Dear Lord, I do not ask
To give me some high work of Thine,
Some noble calling, or some wondrous task;
Give me a little hand to hold in mine;
Give me a little child to point the way
Along the pleasant path that leads to Thee;
Give me two shining eyes Thy face to see.
I do not ask that I may ever stand
Among the wise, the worthy, or the great;
I only ask that softly, hand in hand,
A child and I may enter at the gate.

—ANONYMOUS

XIII

LOOKING THROUGH YOUR CHILDREN'S EYES

To build a happy home requires a lifelong effort. It takes time — much time — to be understanding parents. It is impossible for us to enter into the frustrations and problems of the children without consuming considerable time. To win the confidence of our children and to be in a position to help them, we must take time for comradeship. We must pay the price of time for fellowship and thus give the children the confidence that they know us and that we know them and will face their problems fairly, and not merely dictate answers mechanically. Many homes are unhappy because parents and the children don't understand each other. Too often parents won't pay the price of time for comradeship which is necessary to bridge the one-generation gap between them.

When children do not have confidence in their parents, they either keep their problems to themselves or else go away from home to get help. This is unfortunate, and I think it is largely our fault as parents. We haven't taken the time to prove to the children that we are personally and deeply interested in them. The way we invest our time and our enthusiastic interests tells the children that we have more interest in our work, our organizations or our recreations than we have in them. Certainly as human beings we ought to give at least as much time and thought to training our offspring as we do to the improvement of our crops, pigs or pets. It is sad to say, but many parents can get more concerned over a balky furnace than over a rebellious child. A crop failure brings them more grief than their disobedient children.

Jesus tells us in Matthew 6:19-21, "Lay not up for yourselves treasures upon earth, where moth and rust doth corrupt, and where thieves break through and steal: but lay up for yourselves treasures in heaven, where neither moth nor rust doth corrupt, and where thieves do not break through nor steal: for where your treasure is, there will your heart be also." It is evident that often our hearts have been set on things like clubs, television programs, sports and money rather than our family's welfare. We have had little or no time to enter into the lives of our children and to strengthen the ties of comradeship.

This testimony of failure from one father could be given by a host of others. He says, "I had always had some religion about me. It had never been used very much, but when our boy got beyond advice, persuasion, and punishment I began to look to God to save him, but I meant to help.

"I planned to go out with our boy and be his companion — *when I had time.*

"I resolved to attend church services regularly and take him with me — *when I had time.*

"I hoped to interest him in young people's societies — *when I had time.*

"I promised myself that I would take him into my confidence and talk to him as every father should talk to his son — *when I had time.*

"But I was immersed in business."

This father also said that in the past twenty years, for every one thought he had about his son, he had one hundred thoughts about his business. No wonder such parents are more of a success in business than they are in rearing a family for God.

A farmer and a gardener know that they will never get a crop by sitting in the living room reading. They know that God alone will not operate the farm. It takes a combined effort. In the same way God must be able to work through the parents to accomplish eternal spiritual results in the family.

To build a happy home, parents must remember also that every year is important. We cannot postpone training our children until we have time or until we have all our debts paid. We need to capitalize on daily and hourly opportunities for teaching and companionship. Present opportunities when they are gone never return for us. And they are gone forever.

Someone has said, "Let a child run until he is six and you will never catch him." We dare not put off the task of training our children until a time more convenient to us. Our responsibilities begin as soon as our children are born and last as long as we live, and at no time are they more important than the first fifteen years of their lives. We probably have our greatest opportunities to mold their characters and to influence them before they are ten. Keep it in mind that during the most plastic period of a child's life, the child has comparatively few contacts with persons other than members of the family. Therefore, life in the home is perhaps the most potent factor in the forming of character and personality. Our character as parents and the atmosphere we develop in the home become important because so much more is caught by our children than is taught them.

Now let us look at a number of pointers that will help us as parents to understand our children and their problems. To build happy homes we need to do all we can to foster the confidence of our children in us and then with an intelligent, spiritual approach, help the children through their formative years.

1. First, we need to help our children feel that problems are not sin, but normal signs of development. I have felt in the past that parents and church leaders have discouraged young people from sharing their problems with them because when youth did, they were made to feel wicked or stupid for having had the problems. This is definitely a mistake. No one has all the answers; everyone has problems and the door should always be held wide open by those who can give them the best answers. As parents we should make our children feel that problems are normal and signs of growth and that we welcome their sharing their problems with us. Regardless of how serious the problem is, the child should be made glad that he shared his problem. If we have a startled or painful reaction or make them feel foolish or ignorant, they will likely not come to us with other problems.

2. As parents we must be sympathetic and understanding with the children.

Remember that we are twenty-five or more years older than they are. They belong to another generation. Their environment and problems are somewhat different from what ours were at their age. Also keep in mind the characteristics of their age, because at some periods children don't even understand themselves. We must take into account their physical, social and spiritual development and not judge them on the basis of our maturity and experience. We must try to remember how we felt and the attitudes and ideas we had when we were young. This will help us to deal with the problems of the children in a way that will win their confidence and will in the end give us a happier home.

3. We must remember that the problem or problems of

the child are likely insignificant to us but very, very important to him. It is possible that his problem has caused him loss of sleep and is constantly on his mind. Therefore, as parents we must face the issue with seriousness and make the child feel that we are giving his problem priority and due consideration. To pass it by lightly or to laugh it off will discourage him from coming to you when the next difficulty arises. We must be sensitive to their feelings and convictions.

4. A problem remains a problem in the mind of a child until he has a satisfying answer. No matter how clear or easy the answer is for us, unless the child sees the answer, he still has the problem. We must work in love and patience, for if our answers and suggestions don't register with the child's mind and heart, he will leave us, taking his problem along. It is important that we keep trying to help the child until we have gotten the answer across. However, this doesn't need to be accomplished all in one session.

5. If we do a poor job in helping the child, we have increased his frustration. We must help the child sympathetically and intelligently. We dare not bluff nor use undue pressure. If we don't know, let's tell him so and try to find the answer by the next time.

If the child feels that we are not fair or that our arguments are weak and biased, he will think our position is wrong or else we would have better arguments or answers. Remember, a child at six has just as quick perception as a man; children are not easily fooled. Take time to give good, honest and intelligent answers.

6. Finally, we ought to help our children with a positive approach. Too often we are negative in our decisions and suggestions. Let me illustrate.

A girl who had recently become a Christian asked her pastor if she must now give up the commercial movies. He suggested that she clip out all the newspaper ads about movies for two weeks and then they would look at their advertising program and decide if the movies were helpful to Christians.

The young lady clipped the newspaper ads but was ashamed to view them with her pastor. She handed them to her pastor in a sealed envelope and said she was convinced that movies did not honor God and were not helpful for Christians.

This pastor was wise; he used a positive approach. We will help our children most and retain their confidence best by approaching their problems in a positive, constructive way.

Building a happy home involves diligent effort, careful planning and spiritual consecration on our part. The stream will rise no higher than its source. What we put into our family life will determine to a great extent our results.

Jesus said, "Where your treasure is, there will your heart be also." Again He said, "Seek ye first the kingdom of God, and his righteousness; and all these things shall be added unto you."

To build happy homes as parents, we must be faithful Christians, putting first things first in our program and intelligently entering into the lives and problems of our children.

XIV

MAKING YOUR HOME ATTRACTIVE

My father-in-law is a minister of the Gospel. Some years ago his children and their families came home to attend a church wedding of a relative.

After lunch the children went outside to play while the ladies washed dishes. As father was to officiate at the wedding, he and Mother were leaving earlier.

When they got to their car, they found it full of grandchildren. After the car was cleared of the little folks, they discovered that the key was missing. After a long hunt and much questioning, one of my little boys admitted that he had stuck it down into the door, alongside of the window glass. We couldn't find a second set of keys, and so they finally had to go in another car. The folks were behind schedule and this made it quite frustrating. After all, it's not good for the minister to be late at a wedding.

That evening after the children were in bed, the other members of the family were having a snack in the dining room. My wife said, "Daddy, I was glad for your kind comments about children in your wedding sermon today. I was afraid you wouldn't feel that way after your experience with the grandchildren in your car this afternoon." Then her father said, "Now, Grace, don't read the Scriptures wrong. The Bible says, 'Lo, children are an heritage of the Lord: and the fruit of the womb is his reward. . . . . Happy is the man that hath his quiver full of them.' The

Bible doesn't say, 'Happy is the man that hath his flivver full of them.'" I guess it does make a difference, but I find that if you have a quiver full of children you finally get a flivver full, too.

More seriously, large families are fun and usually children from such integrate into society better because they have had to share in the struggles of the family. In a big family one gets less personal attention and learns to make his own decisions and has to help himself and others earlier in life. There is much hard work in rearing a family, but it is happy and rewarding work if Christ is at the controls. If you want to build a happy home, then plan for a number of children in the family.

As parents, we need children in our homes for our good. They help to make us better men and women. We are better prepared to meet the issues of life if we have had the responsibilities of rearing a family. The cares and responsibilities that come in having a family are not to be compared with the happiness and rewards one receives. Children in your home will help to make it happy because God ordained that children should be a part of the home.

While I was serving on the staff of a young people's summer camp a few years ago, one of the fellows came and poured out his heart to me. He didn't want to go home. He was unhappy there and when away from it, he never had a tug to go back. He despised his father because he was unkind to the family and constantly mocked the boy. There always seemed to be a tension when his father was around. The boy was in deep despair because he knew he had wrong attitudes. He wanted help.

This was indeed a tragedy, but I am sure this picture could be duplicated many times over. There are many young people today who don't enjoy being at home. The good times they have are all outside the home. This ought not to be. If we want to build happy homes, then as parents we must make our homes attractive. It is the responsibility and duty of parents to so plan and conduct family life that the children enjoy coming home and being at home.

The Bible says in Colossians 3:21, "Fathers, provoke not your children to anger, lest they be discouraged." And again in Ephesians 6:4 we read, "And, ye fathers, provoke not your children to wrath: but bring them up in the nurture and admonition of the Lord." I am confident that many of the problems we are having with delinquent juveniles these days are the failures of parents to provide a happy and well-planned home life.

Our whole economy militates against having activities together as a family. So often we have such a high standard of living that mother works away from home to help pay bills. Then when she comes home, she is tired but has duties waiting for her. This creates strain, tension and sharp words. In the evening when happy family activities should take place, then mother's energy is spent and pressing home duties don't permit them. Keep in mind there are some things in life worth a lot more than anything money can buy. Don't let the money god rob you of some of life's greatest treasures. Take time to enjoy your children and to teach them the Word of God. All too soon your opportunity to build their character will be gone. If you take time to be a godly mother, your children will call you blessed and you will have the memory of having served God in the rearing of your family. That will be worth more than millions of dollars.

The poem called "The Builders" expresses my thought:

> A builder builded a temple;
> He wrought it with grace and skill
> Pillars and doors and arches,
> All fashioned to work his will.

Men said, as they saw its beauty,
  "It shall never know decay;
Great is thy skill, O builder!
  Thy fame shall endure for aye."

A mother builded a temple
  With loving and infinite care,
Planning each arch with patience,
  Laying each stone with prayer.
None praised her unceasing efforts,
  None knew of her wondrous plan
For the temple the mother builded
  Was unseen by the eyes of man.

Gone is the builder's temple—
  Crumbled into the dust;
Low lies each stately pillar,
  Food for consuming rust.
But the temple the mother builded
  Will last while the ages roll,
For that beautiful unseen temple
  Was a child's immortal soul.

—AUTHOR UNKNOWN

In these days swing shifts and irregular working schedules prevent wholesome activities. In addition we have so many engagements, meetings and spare-time activities that home life gets the time that is left, which isn't much. We are always rushing through the evening meal getting ready to go somewhere. It's not hard to find some place to go every night in the week. Parents, I believe this is a crime against our children. We must recognize that our homes and families are important and we should plan family nights. We need the conviction that our families are of great importance; then they will get priority on our busy schedules. I even believe it is legitimate to skip some meetings at the church for family life if the church plans something for every night in the week. Few things, if any, are more important than wholesome family activities, and there are no substitutes for them.

Today there are all kinds of clubs, societies, associations and organizations for each member of the family to join. Many of them are fine and have good objectives, but they are robbing families of home life, and therefore the total result may be a curse rather than a help.

Another trick of Satan to keep us from building happy spiritual homes is to provide many forms of entertainment for all members of the family. Movies, television, parties, entertainments, commercial sports and other amusements of all kinds have been bidding for the family's time and money and with much success. And many of these have been a real detriment spiritually because of their appeal to lust. In addition, they have been taking time which the family should have used for their spiritual, social and work projects.

We are being challenged to make our homes attractive so that the family will enjoy staying at home. The world is bidding for our children; we must make sure that home life will be happy and constructive. This takes planning, effort and time, and most of us don't seem to be willing to pay that price. Either we are too busy, don't love our children enough, or else fail to see the importance of home life in building Christian character in our children.

Do you know what most of us do to ease our consciences? We know we ought to spend more time with our families, but we are too busy with other organizational duties and so we buy "things" to make up for our lack of fellowship. As we have more money than time, we try to ease our guilty feeling by buying "things" for our children to retain their friendship. May God forgive us for this. Our children need us. *All* the gifts that money can buy can't do for them what they need. Most of our children are given too many things;

they are spoiled and don't know the value of a dollar. We rob our children by withholding from them some of our time and then we substitute a program of what money can buy and that only does more damage. I can't emphasize too much the fact that our children need us and our personal fellowship. This is a great secret for happy home building. If we are too busy to teach, train, work and play with our children, then we will reap a harvest of regret in a few years. To fail in building Christian character in the children is to fail forever, because they are young only once and the time when they are pliable and easy to mold is short.

We need to spend time and energy planning a family program that is not only interesting but constructive. We know the world's attractions will never teach God's Word and Christian principles to our children; if we don't get it done in our homes, it will likely never get done.

Do your children have a happy home life? Or do you work so hard making money that you never feel like having a good time with the children? This is a serious mistake. As parents we ought to provide recreation for our children at home and ought to participate with them. For our good and their good we ought to play games with our family. It builds confidence and makes a contact that parents can get in no other way.

As parents, we can have invaluable contacts with our children by helping them start and develop hobbies. It takes time, to be sure, but the time used in family recreation and hobbies will never be regretted. These are necessary for the children and will form a valuable tie with them. This is a needful connection with the family to help parents in family discipline and training. It also is a time when one can teach the meaning of spiritual truth. We need to show our children that one can be a good Christian and be wholesome. They need to know that being a Christian is not only going to church and prayer meeting, but it is a rounded and happy life, a good time in the legitimate and wholesome things.

We can help build happy homes with an interesting family program. Such things as happy surprises, family contests and work projects are invaluable in happy home building. Also a good family spirit is developed when the family works together to help make others happy.

For happiness in the home we need to champion the cause of Christ, and the spiritual activities in the home need to be happy occasions. Our children need to see that Christ has priority in our lives and that we are entirely consecrated to His cause. The children will soon discover how important Jesus, the church and the Bible are to us. We can stimulate their faith and build Christian character in them by living a wholesome and happy Christian life with them. May God help us to do just that. We cannot build happy homes with substitutes.

XV

MAKING FAMILY WORSHIP MEANINGFUL

I was sitting in a convention in Cleveland, Ohio, several years ago when I was called aside and informed that my father had been killed a few hours earlier in an automobile accident. In a moment of time he left us and went to be with our Heavenly Father – a glorious exchange for a child of God.

My father was a florist. For perhaps twenty-five years he delivered his flowers to a neighboring city several times a week. Not too long before Father's death, he and I were traveling together in my car; we were on the road that he had traveled often on his flower deliveries. About two miles from his home we rounded a bend in the road and then he said, "At this turn in the road I always begin a prayer of thanksgiving for another safe trip and for my family." He said, "I don't know when I began doing this, but I started it many years ago."

Mother told me that my father knelt beside his bed and prayed before leaving home the morning of his accident, as was always his practice.

I was born in a home of praying parents. We had family worship in our home regularly. We had prayer before each meal, and many times I came upon Mother and Father in private prayer. I shall treasure all my life the spiritual aspects of our home life. It has had a profound effect upon me and has been an invaluable spiritual benefit to me.

You know, if you want to build a happy home, prayer must be a part of your regular family program. There are no substitutes for it, and it is an inheritance that every child deserves. In fact, it is a responsibility God has placed upon us as parents. The Bible says, "And, ye fathers, provoke not your children to wrath: but bring them up in the nurture and admonition of the Lord" (Ephesians 6:4).

In the first chapter of I Samuel we learn some reasons why Samuel of the Old Testament became a spiritual giant. Verses 3 and 7 tell us that his father and mother were regular churchgoers. Not only did the parents attend the religious services regularly but they also took the family along. In verse 21 we read, "And the man Elkanah, and *all his house*, went up to offer unto the Lord the yearly sacrifice, and his vow."

Another spiritual asset that the Prophet Samuel had as a child was praying parents. In verses 10, 11 and 27 we are told that his mother prayed and made vows to her Lord. She knew how to pray and get results. Also in verse 19 we learn that family worship was practiced in their home. The verse says, "And they rose up in the morning early, and worshiped before the Lord. . . ."

What kind of spiritual heritage are you giving your children? As parents we are to be leaders in spiritual things at home. Does your family program include churchgoing, family worship, private prayers and conversation about the Bible? These are important for happy home building.

Several years ago while I was preaching in Alabama, the Spirit of God dealt severely with a middle-aged man. He finally yielded his life to Christ and was saved. After I dismissed the congregation several nights later, he came to me and said, "I'm ashamed to tell you, but I'm forty-three years of age and my children have never heard their daddy pray." He said further, "If God gives me the privilege of having my children home just once more, they will hear me pray." God granted his request and he fulfilled his promise. Family worship became a regular feature of his home. He became a faithful Christian father.

Have your children heard you pray? They should have. In fact, they should hear you pray regularly in family worship. They should often hear you pray for them. It will help to build their character in a way that teaching and discipline can not.

Someone has said, "The family that prays together, stays together." How true that is! Prayer in the presence of each other and for each other has a binding, strengthening and cleansing effect. Jesus said one time, "For where two or three are gathered together in my name, there am I in the midst of them" (Matthew 18:20). Thus when a family gathers to pray, Jesus is in the midst. How needful and wonderful to have Jesus in the middle of your family!

Having a regular family altar, as family worship may be called, is another law for building a happy home.

Do you have family worship in your home? Many homes do not, but not because they don't believe in the practice. They are too busy; it doesn't fit into their program. But to me that is not a justifiable excuse, except for a few times that are exceptions. It may seem that there is no time for some of these most important things in life; we have to take time for them. They may not easily fit into our schedules, but we have to make them fit. As parents it becomes our duty to put first things first. We dare not let the good become the enemy of the best. Many parents would be a lot happier today if they had sacrificed a little profit and had had family worship instead. Now their children have grown up and are gone and oh, the heartache they have caused! The fertile period to mold the character of their children is gone. Oh, yes, they have money in their old age, but how gladly they would exchange it for Christian, parent-honoring children! But they can't; their best opportunities for child training are gone forever, and neither money, tears nor high position can change the picture. Remember, you must take time for family worship in the home. You may have to sacrifice something else, but it will be worth it.

An important matter in making family worship a success is the way it is conducted. It should be a happy time. Parents, we are going to get out of family worship for ourselves and our children what we put into it. The family altar to be a real success must be planned. Someone must give it thought and make preparation. In many homes family worship is unpopular with the children because it is unplanned. No one makes an effort to gear it to the children's level and interest. Don't expect the children to enjoy it if it is only a cold mechanical routine in the schedule. Take time to relate it to the life and experience of the children. They deserve to have family worship conducted in a manner that is helpful and meaningful to them. We plan our work, our vacations and our recreation. Why not plan for the more important experience of family worship?

Let's look at some of the mechanics of a successful family worship experience:

1. When Should It Be Held?
   a. At a time most convenient to all.
   b. When the least pressure for time is on; we should not feel rushed.
   c. The time should be regular. If left for open time, it will be omitted too often.
   d. The morning is preferable.

In the morning we have the clearest minds and can worship best. It is also helpful to start the day together as a family. It is valuable to begin each day by praying for each other. It has a strengthening effect for the day and reminds us that we are walking with God.

2. Where Should It Be Held?

Many people have it just before or after a meal around the table. This is only second best, I believe. If it is before the meal, the little folks are hungry and the sight of good food causes them to be impatient and restless. It's hard to concentrate in the presence of food with an empty stomach. Also the pressure of time is on them because the food is getting overdone on the stove or else cold on the table.

If you eat first and stay sitting at the table for worship, then the sight of dirty dishes may spoil the occasion for mother and the girls. They have a constant reminder of a job awaiting them. At the end of a meal the table is soiled from eating and it is not convenient to lay your songbooks or Bibles on it.

The best system, if it can be worked out, is to eat breakfast and then retire to the living room or library for the family worship period. This setting will be more relaxing and conducive to worship.

3. How Should It Be Conducted?
   a. Plan the schedule for a week or month in advance and post it.
   b. Variety is important—do not always have the same routine. Have the unexpected at times.
   c. It should provide some spiritual help for every member of the family.
   d. All should participate.

Sing together; take turns in reading verses or read in unison; each person can offer a prayer, etc.

4. Suggestions for Variety of Program.
   a. Spend the entire period singing with perhaps one prayer at the end.
   b. Sing one song and spend the entire period in special

prayer. Let each person give several prayer requests and discuss them. It is often good to share several requests for each person to remember in prayer.

c. Memorize passages of Scripture together.
d. Read about, discuss and pray for special programs or projects that are in the church papers.
e. Have a dedication service for your new house, new car, new baby, etc.
f. Make one or two of the children responsible to plan and conduct the period. Notify them at least several days ahead and give each child an opportunity. They will enjoy it and it will be good for them.
g. Let several of the family dramatize a Bible story without words and let the rest try to guess what story it is.
h. Have your guests – missionaries, evangelists, ministers and Christian workers – conduct the family worship occasionally. You get new ideas and the children have real faces in mind when you pray for these people.
i. Plan for special spiritual projects.
   (1) How family tithes should be divided.
   (2) Christmas bundles for overseas.
   (3) Christmas boxes for needy in the community.
   (4) How to help the sick or needy in the community.

5. Materials to Use.
   a. Songbooks – hymnals as well as children's songbooks.
   b. Bibles.
   c. Bible story books.
   d. Devotional books or magazines.
   e. Prayer lists or guides.

Family worship can be enjoyable and anticipated by the children if we parents put forth effort to make it so. We will reap spiritual benefits in the family worship periods in the proportion that we take time and thought in planning them.

Start right away on a good daily family worship period in your home. Don't grow old and wish you had put first things first in your home when the children were growing up. Rather, as you grow old, and rejoice that you took the time to give spiritual things first place in your home and family life. When the children are growing up we are setting the stage considerably for happiness or unhappiness in our old age. All too soon the children will be grown and gone from us; then we will have our memories to live with.

Give Christ first place in your lives and homes and you will know the greatest secret for building a happy home.